A FATHER'S GIFT

A FATHER'S GIFT

Lessons from Proverbs

Kenneth B. Wingate

THE BANNER OF TRUTH TRUST

THE BANNER OF TRUTH TRUST
3 Murrayfield Road, Edinburgh EH12 6EL, UK
P.O. Box 621, Carlisle, PA 17013, USA

*

© Kenneth B. Wingate 2009

*

ISBN-13: 978 1 84871 050 4

*

Typeset in 11/15 Adobe Caslon Pro at
the Banner of Truth Trust, Edinburgh

Printed in the U.S.A. by
Versa Press, Inc.,
East Peoria, IL

To Cathy,
My greatest gift from the Lord:

*Many women have done excellently,
but you surpass them all.*

To Miriam, Bryan and Catharine:

*May God give you wisdom to walk in his ways
and the grace to live life abundantly.*

Contents

FOREWORD

There is a long and honourable tradition in the English-speaking world of lawyers who have distinguished themselves not only in their profession as attorneys, but in the exemplary way in which they have served their cities, states and nations with great distinction.

The southern states of what is now the United States of America have been marked by men in the legal profession who have been distinguished by their Christian character, their role in the church, their leadership in their home, and all of this grounded in their love for the ministry of God's Word and their disciplined personal reading and study of it. Their Christian faith has driven their professional lives simply because faith in Christ has been the driving force of the whole of their lives.

Kenneth Wingate belongs to this noble company. His calling is to practice law in Columbia, South Carolina. His passion is to love and serve the Lord Jesus Christ. He has done this with grace and thoroughness in the concentric spheres of his life: family, church, profession, city and state.

A Father's Gift gives hints of these circles of life without detailing the extent to which its author has been trusted to serve in them with distinction. It has been written, essentially, for his own family—not least for himself as a means of clarifying the responsibilities and privileges he has shared with his wife Cathy for the Christian nurturing of their children. It is in the truest sense a father's gift to his own family, and our privilege as readers to be able to eavesdrop on the counsel Ken has mined from the wisdom of God's Word, and especially from the book of Proverbs. The fruit of all this, as I am able to testify from personal friendship—although perhaps Miriam, Bryan, and Catharine would rather I left their names out of this foreword!—is the reproduction, by God's Word and Spirit, of Christian character—and 'characters'.

Many young parents today are beside themselves with anxieties about their children, and, sadly, confusion too about how to nurture them. The ongoing addiction of our times to the heresy of modernity ('the latest book, or guru, is likely to have it right') and its proud rejection—and ignorance—of the tested and tried wisdom of the past, inevitably leads to dysfunction in home and family life. Sadly, the older, wiser counsel of God's Word—and especially of the book of Proverbs—is unknown or neglected. Yet Proverbs was composed specifically as a manual for home and family instruction, and to prepare us for life in the world. It is a divinely given handbook to help parents. Indeed it appears to begin, as Old Testament theologian Bruce Waltke has insightfully shown, with a series of basic 'father-son' talks (easily translated into father-daughter or mother-daughter talks!). These are then followed by a miniature library of wisdom expressed in memorable —and easily memorized—ways.

Proverbs—and Ken Wingate following it—does not provide a mechanical, formalized, slot machine approach to building Christian character (do X and Y is guaranteed). Rather it shows us the way to possess the jewel of all jewels in a well-adorned life: wisdom that is rooted in the knowledge of, and reverential love for, God. 'The beginning of wisdom is this: get wisdom, and whatever you get, get insight' (*Prov.* 4:7). From chapter 1 these parent-child talks point us to their fruit in manly godliness and their expression in the godly femininity with which the book closes in chapter 31. That is why Proverbs has proved to be worth its weight in gold in every age and culture. Ken Wingate now brings it into our needy culture, and I for one am grateful to him for sharing his gift as a father with other fathers—and mothers, and sons and daughters too.

Here then is a book for parents to read on their own; for teenagers to read on their own; for parents and teenagers, who are willing to take the family challenge, to read round the table after dinner or on other occasions. It points us to God's way. It promises us God's grace. What could be better for us than that?

SINCLAIR B. FERGUSON
First Presbyterian Church,
Columbia,
South Carolina

Author's Preface

It was Christmas morning, 1996. Our extended family—three generations of Wingates and Edwards—had gathered at the farm we call 'Limerick'. Fifteen people, three Labrador Retrievers, and a cat scurried around the festively decorated farmhouse. A fire crackled in the fireplace. I vividly remember every detail of that cold, beautiful, noisy morning.

The children were excited, gift wrapping was flying, dogs' tails were wagging, Christmas music was playing. But in the midst of the revelry something was missing. Somehow the nicely wrapped gifts, though beautiful, seemed a little empty. The real agenda of the day was not yet accomplished.

I went for a solitary walk in the woods, and as I walked I prayed out loud: 'Lord, what is the best gift I can give my children for Christmas? What present will truly last?' My immediate impression was, 'Write them a book on life's most important lessons.'

In the days and weeks that followed, I searched the Scriptures, asking myself what lessons a father ought to pass on to his children. I kept going back to this passage from Proverbs:

> Hear, my son, your father's instruction, and forsake not your mother's teaching, for they are a graceful garland for your head and pendants for your neck (1:8-9).

What instructions? What teaching? Thus I began sifting through and summarizing the lessons of Proverbs. What are its key principles? What words of wisdom did the father impart to his sons and daughters?

The longer I've studied, the more I am captivated by the practical wisdom of the book of Proverbs. It reveals the path to abundant life—and that is precisely the gift I want to give my children!

Twelve years and many life events later, here is the gift I've been making. It is really a personal gift for my three children, Miriam, Bryan and Catharine, but I am more than happy to share it with anyone who cares to eavesdrop on our conversation.

KEN WINGATE
Columbia,
South Carolina

1

Abundant Life:
Introduction to Proverbs

I came that they may have life and have it abundantly.
(John 10:10)

We all want the most out of life. But which path leads to the abundance Jesus promised?

For some people, abundance is measured in dollars. Long hours, hard work, and doing whatever it takes to get ahead becomes their path of choice. For others, attaining power, making a name for themselves, or maximizing leisure and pleasure is their goal. Perhaps many have no specific aim but just float down the river of life, hoping to avoid the rocks. Each preferred path leads to a multitude of consequences. But at the end of the day, what really satisfies the soul? How do we make the *best* choices in life?

The Bible teaches that God created us with a specific goal for our life. Finding the path that leads to that goal, and sticking to it, is what will make us truly happy. True success in life means faithfully fulfilling that purpose. And that is what Scripture is all about—it is the only trustworthy guide that will faithfully direct us along the whole of life's way. God told Joshua,

> This Book of the Law shall not depart from your mouth, but you shall meditate on it day and night, so that you may be careful to do according to all that is written in it. For then you will make your way prosperous, and then you will have good success (*Josh.* 1:8).

The psalmist wrote, 'Your word is a lamp to my feet and a light to my path' (*Psa.* 119:105). But of all the books in the Bible, Proverbs supplies the most practical advice on choosing the right path.

The ancient Hebrews had a word for the ability to make the best choices in life: *wisdom*. Wisdom is much more than the possession of knowledge or intelligence—it is living life skilfully. The wise person makes the right choices, says the right words, spends time and resources on the things that matter most. The wise person is blessed—he enjoys God's presence and approval.

The wise person also has the right perspective on life—he has a bird's-eye view of the maze. It is this heavenly perspective that allows us to pick carefully our way around obstacles, avoid pitfalls, identify and then reach the right goals. Wisdom is the ability to see life as God sees it.

The book of Proverbs is a compendium of wisdom—a collection of carefully worded sayings intended to instruct the young, remind the forgetful, and warn the naïve in the ways of life. Proverbs is a road map for life. My purpose in writing this little book is to summarize some of the key principles found in the book of Proverbs. My desire is that these simple words of spiritual wisdom will become the foundation upon which my own children will build their lives. For knowing the living and true God and humbly walking through life in fellowship with him is the only lasting measure of success and the source of real satisfaction in this world.

President Theodore Roosevelt once said, 'Character, in the long run, is the decisive factor in the life of an individual and of nations alike.' Good character grows out of thousands of minute-by-minute choices that favour wisdom over folly. Sadly, our modern culture much prefers personality to character. Personality is a divine quality, for God created us as individuals. Each one of us is a person created by God—unique in appearance, voice, fingerprints, thoughts, and opinions. But true individualism means having the freedom to serve God uniquely, not the freedom to live independently from God's guidance or control. The Bible teaches us that mankind's primary purpose in life is to know, honour, and enjoy the Creator. Individualism is necessary to fulfil that purpose, but it means freedom to do the right thing—not freedom to do whatever we might choose.

There are moral laws just as there are physical laws in this universe. An object dropped from a table will fall to the floor thanks to the law of gravity. Anyone who ignores the law of gravity does so at his own risk! Likewise, this universe has its moral laws. A person who ignores God's moral laws also does so at his own risk. Disregard for God's laws is called sin in Scripture (the Greek word for sin basically means to 'miss the mark', to 'fall short of the goal'). Our culture scoffs at the concept of sin. The vast majority today believe there is no such thing as absolute right or wrong. For them right and wrong are relative concepts which depend on life's various situations. Yet Scripture teaches that there are truths which are absolute and eternal and behavioural guidelines which have been ordained by the Creator. The wise person follows God's instructions, but the fool disregards them and follows his own desires. The wise will find abundance, but the foolish will find emptiness. Sin—the conscious choice to depart from God's path and to go our own way—may seem enticing, but it leads to destruction.

Which Gate Marks the Path?

Scripture sets before us two paths. The path of self-reliance leads ultimately to destruction and ruin, whereas the path of God-reliance leads to abundance. 'Trust in the Lord with all your heart, and do not lean on your own understanding. In all your ways acknowledge him, and he will make straight your paths' (*Prov.* 3:5-6). The choice of which path to follow makes all the difference in the world. 'There is a way that seems right to a man, but its end is the way to death' (14:12).

Life's two paths—self-reliance and God-reliance—are each entered through their respective gates.

> Enter by the narrow gate. For the gate is wide and the way is easy that leads to destruction, and those who enter by it are many. For the gate is narrow and the way is hard that leads to life, and those who find it are few (*Matt.* 7:13-14).

What is the 'narrow' gate? In his parable of the sheepfold, Jesus said, 'I am the door. If anyone enters by me, he will be saved and will go in and out and find pasture' (*John* 10:9). On another occasion he said, 'I am the way, and the truth, and the life. No one comes to the Father except through me' (14:6). The 'broad' gate is easy to find because it marks the path of self-reliance. It is the easiest gate to enter because it stands at the head of the most natural path for us to choose, the wide way that never demands the sacrifice of self as one's master. Doing whatever pleases self is life's easy path, but, according to the Lord Jesus, it 'leads to destruction'.

Where Does the Path Begin?

Every journey begins with a single step, and knowing the living God is the first step on the way to an abundant life. 'The fear of the Lord is the beginning of wisdom, and the knowledge of the

Holy One is insight' (*Prov.* 9:10). Our primary goal in life must be to live in the fear of the Lord, to know the Holy One. That is what Proverbs teaches us. Derek Kidner writes: 'a sense of purpose and calling lifts the teaching of Proverbs above the pursuit of success or tranquillity, clear of the confines of . . . dry moralism, into the realm of knowing the living God "in all (one's) ways".'[1] As the *Westminster Shorter Catechism* says, 'Man's chief end is to glorify God, and to enjoy him forever.' Knowledge of our Creator and the way he has ordered his world is not only the means to successful living, but knowing and enjoying him is in itself the ultimate goal.

What does Proverbs mean when it says that this enjoyable relationship begins with 'fearing the Lord'? In part the fear of the Lord means awe and respect, but it also means much more than that. It is an awareness that God is present with us, watching everything we do, say, and even think. 'For a man's ways are before the eyes of the LORD, and he ponders all his paths' (5:21). The Bible teaches clearly that God is an ever-present spirit who knows everything that happens. He is everywhere at once, and nothing escapes his attention. This is a great comfort for many and a great problem for others. 'The eyes of the LORD are in every place, keeping watch on the evil and the good' (15:3).

For the person who submits to God's authority, the awareness of his watching eye is a great comfort. Lion cubs play happily under the watchful eye of the mighty lioness, even though danger may be lurking nearby. Her attentive presence ensures protection and peace. Likewise, no matter how dark the night or how far from home we may be, we are never alone, for 'the LORD of hosts is with us' (*Psa.* 46:7).

Awareness of God's presence also brings respect for his authority over us. This is the 'fear of the Lord' for the believer—a healthy

---

[1] Derek Kidner, *Proverbs: An Introduction and Commentary,* (Inter-Varsity Press, 1964), p. 21.

balance between fearing God's discipline if we sin and respecting and enjoying his presence. A sense of God's approval grows with the awareness of his watchful eye upon us and a desire to please him. As we make progress in the way of faith the sense of his presence grows. 'But the path of the righteous is like the light of dawn, which shines brighter and brighter until full day' (4:18). As a child of the king we have free access to the throne room of heaven. We live life daily in God's presence—respecting his authority over us, willingly obeying him and serving him with great joy.

How can we practically experience this fear of the Lord? By talking to God out loud or in the quiet recesses of the heart. By counting our blessings and thanking him for all he has done. By reflecting on his mighty deeds and his sustaining grace. By pondering the wonders and mysteries of his beautiful creation. By picturing him as a loving father who delights in the children he has redeemed at such great cost to himself. By filling our minds with Scripture, with the biographies of great believers, and with other inspirational literature. By not allowing the mindless, incessant drone of television, iPods or the Internet drown the soul's quest for fellowship with the Creator. His is the still, small voice, and it can be easily drowned out by the frantic clamour of daily life.

Melts in Your Heart, not in Your Head

The New Testament sheds more light on how we find wisdom and life: 'If the Spirit of him who raised Jesus from the dead dwells in you, he who raised Christ Jesus from the dead will also give life to your mortal bodies through his Spirit who dwells in you' (*Rom.* 8:11). It is not head knowledge (an accumulation of facts and experiences), but heart knowledge that makes us wise and gives us life. We might live as long as Methuselah yet never become wise, because our natural, self-reliant ways of life and thought are so very different from God's ways. The Apostle Paul spent his early years studying and training his mind in the Law, but it was not until he had an encounter with Jesus on the road to Damascus that the light dawned on him. A personal encounter with the living God instantly transformed and re-ordered his great store of knowledge. In later years he wrote to the church:

> and my speech and my message were not in plausible words of wisdom, but in demonstration of the Spirit and of power, that your faith might not rest in the wisdom of men but in the power of God . . . Now we have received not the spirit of the world, but the Spirit who is from God, that we might understand the things freely given us by God. And we impart this in words not taught by human wisdom but taught by the Spirit, interpreting spiritual truths to those who are spiritual. The natural person does not accept the things of the Spirit of God, for they are folly to him, and he is not able to understand them because they are spiritually discerned (*1 Cor.* 2:4-14).

Proverbs does not give us a book of rules—do's and don'ts—that if followed will win us favour with God. His mercy and favour are freely given to all who simply trust him. Along with forgiveness God also gives us his Spirit to dwell within us, and to change us from the inside out.

Our day to day character and conduct are merely external indicators of the inner condition of our soul. We cannot earn God's favour by doing good things and by acting wisely,: we cannot lift ourselves up by our own boot straps. We cannot win God's favour by being the right kind of person. We must first receive God's grace in Christ Jesus which will bring us into a right relationship with God. That is the first step in the journey to abundant life. Unless we are on that path, with Christ our Saviour, we are not going to fulfil the purpose for which we were created: knowing and enjoying God in all our ways. The great irony is that only in losing ourselves do we find ourselves, together with life's greatest joys.

We Are What We Eat

Our behaviour—what we say and do—comes from what we think. What we think is influenced largely by what we feed our minds. What we read, hear and watch has a profound effect on how we govern and direct our inner emotions and thoughts. We are what we eat!

My assumption is that the Holy Bible is exactly what it claims to be—the inspired word of the God who made us. 'For the word of God is living and active, sharper than any two-edged sword, piercing to the division of soul and of spirit, of joints and of marrow, and discerning the thoughts and intentions of the heart' (*Heb.* 4:12). Therefore, it is the only authoritative guide for life as God intends it. What is further, God gave it to us for the very purpose of instructing us in the proper use and care of our life, something akin to an owner's manual. 'All Scripture is breathed out by God and profitable for teaching, for reproof, for correction, and for training in righteousness, that the man of God may be competent, equipped for every good work' (*2 Tim.* 3:16-17). The Bible is perfectly reliable and inherently profitable for training us—for guiding us along the best path of life.

The *Shorter Catechism* teaches us that the 'Scriptures principally teach what man is to believe concerning God, and what duties God requires of man.' Proverbs is not a book of the Bible that focuses primarily on theology—what we are to believe concerning God—yet it sheds light on two of God's most significant attributes. First, it teaches that God is omniscient, knowing not only our outward behaviour but also our inner thoughts and motives. 'For a man's ways are before the eyes of the Lord, and he ponders all his paths' (5:21). Second, it teaches that God actively guides and protects us, imparting wisdom to those who seek him. 'For the LORD gives wisdom; from his mouth come knowledge and understanding; he stores up sound wisdom for the upright; he is a shield to those who walk in integrity' (2:6-7).

Proverbs' focus falls primarily on the second part of the *Catechism's* answer: the 'duties God requires of man'. What does God require in terms of our attitudes and actions in daily living—the things we value, how we use our time, how we treat our friends and neighbours, how we speak to others, how well we control our appetites, how we manage our finances, etc.? Regarding these important issues Proverbs provides us with a treasure trove of practical wisdom.

To live abundantly we must be people of the Book. The habit of regular Bible reading is foundational to success and fulfilment in life. The more we read, study and memorize Scripture, the more it will shape our worldview and govern our conduct. 'Bind them on your heart always; tie them around your neck. When you walk, they will lead you; when you lie down, they will watch over you; and when you awake, they will talk with you. For the commandment is a lamp and the teaching a light, and the reproofs of discipline are the way of life' (6:21-23).

Let's look at some of the major issues addressed by Proverbs. My hope is that you will keep them continually in mind as you navigate your way. They will guide you into the abundant life.

Key Principle: The 'fear of the LORD' is the first step on the path to abundant life.

2

WEALTH

Wealth: call it finances, money, possessions, things, stuff. We live in a culture obsessed with stuff. How do we keep it in perspective? Proverbs teaches a great deal about wealth—what to do with it and what not to do with it. First, Proverbs teaches the positive side—how we are to obtain, manage and use our possessions. But Proverbs also teaches us the negative side—mistakes to avoid in acquiring and maintaining wealth. The warnings, if examined first, would give the wrong picture, because our Creator intended material things to be enjoyed appropriately and used constructively by us his creatures.

Christ said in the Sermon on the Mount, 'No one can serve two masters, for either he will hate the one and love the other, or he will be devoted to the one and despise the other. You cannot serve God and money' (*Matt.* 6:24). In the original Greek of the New Testament the word translated 'money' (also rendered as 'mammon' in some versions), means our worldly possessions—things we own. By definition, things are lifeless objects. Yet, strangely, wealth and possessions take on a life of their own. Though God intended them to be used by us, these things can sometimes own us. Rather than being our servants, they can become our masters. We must keep wealth in its proper place. We are to use it as an instrument for good; it is never to be master over us.

Hold Material Things Lightly

There is nothing wrong with wealth, so long as we hold it with a loose hand. If the Lord gives us an abundance of wealth, that's great! Use it, enjoy it, share it with gratitude, realizing that one day we will give an account to God for our stewardship. But if the Lord takes the wealth away, we must continue to trust him as a sovereign, loving Father. That which he chooses to place in our hands, whether much or little, is his prerogative.

The basic problem with wealth is that it can give us a false sense of security. The Lord alone should be the centre of our life—it is he who made us and sustains us. If we divert our reliance away from God and trust in our possessions for our security, peace and happiness, we have traded a foundation of rock for one of sand. 'Whoever trusts in his riches will fall' (*Prov.* 11:28).

Nothing is wrong with wealth and possessions, so long as we learn that amassing wealth is the least worthwhile of goals, and that when accumulated, it can be the spoiler of far more important things. 'Better is a little with the fear of the Lord than great treasure and trouble with it' (15:16). Possessions can be like the squeaky wheel that always needs oil. They can distract us with their constant demands.

Another problem associated with material wealth is that it will not last. Proverbs 23:4-5 says, 'Do not toil to acquire wealth; be discerning enough to desist. When your eyes light on it, it is gone, for suddenly it sprouts wings, flying like an eagle toward heaven.'

The Lord often uses wealth to test our hearts. Imagine a large, powerful magnet used to sort a pile of scrap metal. Some of the scrap might be steel, which will be drawn to the magnet. Some might be aluminium, which will not be drawn to the magnet. The operator moves the magnet across the heap to sort it. In a sense, that's what the Lord sometimes does with wealth and possessions. He is testing us, to see if we are drawn to the magnetic allure of riches. Wealth is an instrument which measures the level of trust we have in the Lord. Is our security, satisfaction and sense of self-worth tied to our possessions? Do we love the Giver of all gifts, simply because he is worth loving, or do we love him because of his generous gifts? Contentment with our material possessions is one of the demands the Lord places upon his children.

Cathy's aunt, Deedie Melchers, often says, 'There are two ways to be rich: have much or want little.' The person who wants little has learned the secret of contentment!

Proverbs reminds us to adopt a long-term perspective on our assets and investments. 'Riches do not profit in the day of wrath, but righteousness delivers from death' (11:4). Scripture teaches that we live in two worlds simultaneously. First, we live in the physical world, with the tangible things around us that we can touch, see, hear, smell, and taste. Yet simultaneously there's another world—the spiritual—which is all around us in a different realm. It is not visible, but invisible; not temporal, but eternal. Yet, it is not only equally real, it is more lasting than the physical world. Isaiah revealed this truth from God, saying, 'Lift up your eyes to the heavens, and look at the earth beneath; for the heavens vanish like smoke, the earth will wear out like a garment, and they who dwell in it will die in like manner; but my salvation will be forever' (*Isa.* 51: 6-7).

We look at the sky in its expanse and look at the ground beneath our feet, and they seem so solid and permanent. Yet one day the sky will disappear like a puff of smoke. And one day the earth will wear out like an old garment that has been washed too many times—full of holes and deteriorating. 'But my righteousness will be forever' (*Isa.* 51:8). In other words, the physical realm is passing away, and one day will be destroyed. The spiritual realm will keep on going, and is thus the more real and permanent of our two worlds. Viewed on that dual plane, riches do not profit in the day of wrath. It's like we're in a canoe that is going along a raging river, and suddenly we come to the steep falls and go right over the edge. The world will drop out from under us—then what good is the paddle? Riches will be of no use in the day of wrath.

'Whoever trusts in his riches will fall, but the righteous will flourish like a green leaf' (11:28). Riches can give us a false sense of security in life. If we have a house with a high brick wall, a nice, fat bank account, and a well-funded retirement plan, we begin to feel secure. Nothing can harm us. Yet, Proverbs says those things will fail us, and give us only a false sense of security.

We need to call to mind often that the Lord desires to restore his own image in us, that we might know him, trust him, love him and enjoy him. He is not primarily concerned with our financial security and neither should we be so concerned. The Lord will meet our needs and he uses money as a means for so doing, but the acquisition of wealth, in and of itself, is not part of his agenda for our lives.

The Danger of a Full Freezer

'Do not toil to acquire wealth; be discerning enough to desist. When your eyes light on it, it is gone, for suddenly it sprouts wings, flying like an eagle toward heaven' (23:4-5). Wealth is not permanent. It can vanish like smoke in the air. The Lord teaches us to stand before his sovereign throne with open hands. We are called in all circumstances to enjoy and appreciate the good things the Lord puts in our hands, to thank him for them and to use them for the good of others. And yet, if he chooses to take away these things, we must remain content in such straitened circumstances. Don't cling to wealth.

There is danger in having a full freezer. 'Take care lest you forget the LORD your God . . . lest, when you have eaten and are full and have built good houses and live in them, and when your herds and flocks multiply and your silver and gold is multiplied and all that you have is multiplied, then your heart be lifted up, and you forget the LORD your God, who brought you out of the land of Egypt, out of the house of slavery . . . Beware lest you say in your heart, "My power and the might of my hand have gotten me this wealth."' (*Deut.* 8:11-17). Prosperity can make us think we did it on our own, when in reality we are powerless. Prosperity can be a more trying test of our faith than poverty. The 'self-made man' is prone to believe he is self-sufficient, when in fact he is dependent on God for every breath he draws. How can I be so arrogant as to think that I am worth something because I have a well-paid job and a house, when the Lord could so easily have placed me in circumstances where I had no job, no income, and no ability to earn a living. Don't let prosperity lead you away from trusting in the Lord; prosperity offers only a false security.

In the developed world today, many are artificially insulated from life's ups and downs by various safety nets—homeowner's insurance, health insurance, disability insurance, long-term care insurance, social security and retirement accounts to name but a few. Insuring against unexpected losses is wise, but does not change our fundamental dependence on God to meet our daily needs. 'A rich man's wealth is his strong city, and like a high wall in his imagination' (18:11). The highest walls can fall so quickly. Trust in the Lord alone.

Contentment through Life's Ups and Downs

The Lord takes us through various life experiences—for better and for worse, for richer and for poorer, in sickness and in health. And he frequently takes us through tough financial circumstances too in order to discover on what our trust truly relies.

Think of how the Lord tested Joseph. He started off as the favourite son of his wealthy father, Jacob, who presented him with a rich multi-coloured coat along with all the possessions he could enjoy. Yet, his brothers, irritated by Joseph's boasting, stole his coat, faked his death, and sold him into slavery. Joseph went from prince to pauper in a day. Years later, through his hard work and loyalty, he rose again to prosperity as the chief steward to Potiphar, a wealthy and powerful man in Egypt. Potiphar gave Joseph responsibility over all he owned. But one day Potiphar's wife tried to seduce Joseph. Rather than cheating on his master, Joseph fled the seductive scene. The spurned wife accused Joseph of attempted rape, and he was thrown back into prison. Wealth to poverty to wealth to poverty.

Yet again because of his faithfulness, Joseph rose—not as Jacob's favourite son, not as Potiphar's chief steward, but as the chief advisor to Pharaoh, Ruler of Egypt. And so we see in Joseph's life how the Lord used these times of freedom and captivity, wealth and poverty, to test him and to mature him. And he passed the test with flying colours! Joseph's trust was not in circumstances or possessions, his trust was in the Lord.

Centuries later, the Apostle Paul had a similar experience. In Philippians 4:11 he wrote, 'I have learned in whatever situation I am to be content.' Whether my stomach is full or whether it is empty, whether in times of prosperity or in times of need, I am content in any and every circumstance.

We are to learn that kind of contentment too. We are to trust in the Lord's unchanging goodness and not in the things which we have accumulated. 'The blessing of the Lord makes rich, and he adds no sorrow with it' (*Prov.* 10:22). The one who places his trust in the Lord, in the area of material wealth, is going to have a blessing, a satisfaction, a contentment that brings with it no sorrow, no curse, no burden. 'Better is a little with the fear of the Lord than great treasure and trouble with it' (15:16) 'Better is a little with righteousness than great revenues with injustice' (16:8). 'Better is a dry morsel with quiet than a house full of feasting with strife.' (17:1). Who would not rather eat a stale piece of bread and have a cup of lukewarm water and live in peace and contentment rather than have an abundance of rich food and flowing wine and live in a house full of strife and grief? Which is ultimately the more blessed condition? Better is the little than the much. Better is the contentment than the grief. Better is the righteousness than the wickedness. We are called to be content in all circumstances.

In the early 1980s, the undeveloped Daniel Island near Charleston Harbor was a private hunting preserve owned by the Guggenheim Foundation of New York. Charleston lawyer and foundation trustee, Henry Smythe, often hunted there on weekends. Arriving late at the locked gates one Saturday, long after the other hunters, Henry found the elderly black gentleman who kept the keys, and asked to be admitted. The man was unmoved by his appeal. Frustrated, Henry said, 'I'm Henry Smythe, and I'm the Foundation's lawyer.' Sceptical, the old man stepped back, thoughtfully eyed Henry's beat up old station wagon, and said, 'No sir, that ain't no lawyer car!' So rare was Henry's contentment with an old car that it cost him admission to the hunt!

Honesty—the Only Policy

An often-repeated warning in Proverbs is to avoid fraud or deception in trying to gain material wealth. 'A false balance is an abomination to the Lord, but a just weight is his delight' (11:1). The picture is of a merchant in the marketplace selling grain, and he has a false balance. The set of weights he uses is deceptive; the one-pound weight really weighs fourteen-and-a-half ounces rather than the full sixteen ounces. When the unwary buyer puts down his money for a pound of grain, the merchant deceptively uses the light weight on the scale to pass it off as a full pound's worth. That, says the Scripture, is an abomination to the Lord.

The word 'abomination' in Hebrew cannot be strongly enough translated into the English language. It means wretched to the point of making one gag. God is repulsed by us if we use a false balance and defraud others in our dealings.

Not only does fraud repulse God, but he actively opposes the wrongdoer. 'Wealth gained hastily will dwindle, but whoever gathers little by little will increase it' (13:11). 'Bread gained by deceit is sweet to a man, but afterward his mouth will be full of gravel' (20:17). Fraud actually causes wealth to dwindle! Though stolen bread may taste sweet for a moment, by the time it reaches our stomach it will be as nutritious as a brick! The Lord will not turn a blind eye to it.

How does this apply in my every-day world? What if the rule in my office is 'No personal use of the photocopier'? Yet I think, how much can it possibly cost the owner—maybe a penny a page? So breaking the rule is justified; it's a small thing. It's the big deception that I wouldn't do, right? I would never steal $100 from the petty cash fund, but I'll make the photocopy because there's nothing really wrong. Look at it the other way around. Why would I sell my soul for one cent? Why not count the copies and pay my employer a nickel or a dime rather than cheat? The Lord says be honest, be up front in all our dealings.

'Whoever is greedy for unjust gain troubles his own household, but he who hates bribes will live' (15:27). We can examine our lives and see many ways in which we cut corners or use a sharp pencil to work the arithmetic in our own favour. Yet we are warned about the trouble that brings upon our house.

Corporate America has witnessed many financial train wrecks in the last decade. Executives at WorldCom Inc., the bankrupt telecommunications company, were accused of being co-conspirators in an accounting scandal which overstated profits by $9 billion.[1] Energy giant Enron Corp., when it was forced into bankruptcy, was 'a house of cards, where human error and a culture of ambition, secrecy and greed made collapse inevitable.' Its president 'sponsored and approved accounting and tax gimmicks with private partnerships and funds that contributed billions in improper or questionable earnings.'[2] The resulting collapse cost thousands of employees their jobs and wiped out their life savings.

Similar failures happen daily on a smaller scale. A State Farm insurance agent hatched a scheme to take advantage of his employer's charitable matching-contribution program. The man called fellow agents like Paul Julian of California, asking them to accept $1,000 each from him, and pass the money on to his *alma mater*, Wayne State College in Nebraska. The employer would then match each donation with another $1,000. When 54 contributions went to the same university, State Farm became suspicious. It ultimately fired all 54 agents for defrauding the company by circumventing the program's $1,000 limit. The consequence of a seemingly small decision to help a friend by side-stepping the rules? 'It was a three-minute phone conversation that changed my life', said Julian, as he closed the doors on an insurance business he built over 35 years.[3]

[1] www.etaiwannews.com, September 9, 2002.
[2] www.washingtonpost.com, September 9, 2002.
[3] www.thestate.com, May 3, 1997.

Sometimes the story has a happy ending. Louie Weathersbee of Pickens, South Carolina, thought he had put his briefcase in his truck, but inadvertently left it on his bumper. After driving to work he discovered the briefcase, containing $2,100 in cash, was missing. He began to pray, 'Lord, please let someone find that briefcase. And please let it be someone honest.' Shortly thereafter Irene Revis, 65, and her sister, 72, spotted something on the road, stopped and picked it up. Opening the briefcase and finding the cash, they immediately turned it over to the local sheriff's department. 'It was so refreshing to have a visit like that', said the deputy sheriff. 'O, Lord, I'm so thankful', said Weathersbee, as he gave the sisters a $100 thank-you gift.[4]

Snake Eyes—Double or Nothing

One of the phenomena sweeping our Western culture in recent decades has been gambling. Sports wagering, bingo parlours, Internet and video games, casinos and government-sponsored lotteries are multi-trillion dollar businesses. Ironically, the proceeds of state-sponsored games are typically earmarked for noble causes such as education or services for senior citizens. So what is wrong with rolling the dice and hoping to get lucky?

The primary flaw with such games is that they are misleading to the uninformed. The chance of winning is minuscule (the odds against winning the Powerball jackpot is currently 195,000,000 to 1), yet the advertisements in many places target the poor and uneducated. For them, the possibility of winning is seen as a ticket out of poverty. In this sense, the lottery steals from the poor to give to the rich. 'Whoever oppresses a poor man insults his Maker, but he who is generous to the needy honours him' (14:31).

Another common mistake for habitual gamblers is the desire to

---

[4] www.thestate.com, August 2, 1997.

acquire wealth without labour. The get-rich-quick mentality can become a disincentive to pursue honest work. 'Whoever works his land will have plenty of bread, but he who follows worthless pursuits lacks sense' (12:11). Ironically, sudden wealth, if found, rarely lingers and more rarely satisfies. 'An inheritance gained hastily in the beginning will not be blessed in the end' (20:21). 'A man whose eye is evil hastens after wealth and does not know that poverty will come upon him' (28:22). Don't waste time or money on such 'games'—even the (few) winners are losers.

Due Diligence

Proverbs strongly warns that we must not be lazy or negligent in work or financial matters. 'A slack hand causes poverty, but the hand of the diligent makes rich' (*Prov.* 10:4). As a general rule in life work equals progress, effort equals distance gained. In general terms the Lord provides for us by the use of very ordinary means. It is through the work of our hands that he provides for our material needs. That is why we are not to be negligent in these things. Whatever the Lord has prepared us for, and in whatever circumstances he has placed us, we are to work diligently in order to earn a living. This is a theme that recurs often in the book of Proverbs: 'Whoever works his land will have plenty of bread, but he who follows worthless pursuits lacks sense' (12:11). 'Whoever works his land will have plenty of bread, but he who follows worthless pursuits will have plenty of poverty' (28:19).

After finishing law school in 1986, my first job was at the Mc-Nair Law Firm in Columbia, a firm headed by former South Carolina Governor Robert E. McNair. 'Big Bob', as my young children referred to him, would often say, 'I've worked hard and I've been lucky. But I've noticed that the harder I work, the luckier I get.' The point is well taken. Effort generally yields results.

Some people tire of work easily and want to ease up as soon as it stops being fun. Work stamina is an important thing to acquire. Work will not always be full of excitement and glory. There may or may not be a sense of gratification in the work we do to earn our daily bread. More will be said about that in a later chapter. The point to be made here is that we are to diligently apply our hands to the work that the Lord has put before us. 'A slack hand causes poverty, but the hand of the diligent makes rich' (10:4). 'Whoever is slack in his work is a brother to him who destroys' (18:9). Negligence is no different than outright stealing.

One of the DeHahn family, writing in *Our Daily Bread,* said that when he was a young man he worked on a summer construction job. An older worker, a World War I veteran, said to him one day, 'Young man, when you go to the store and pay for a loaf of bread, what do you expect to receive?' His answer naturally was, 'Well, a loaf of bread. I paid for a loaf, I want a loaf of bread.' The veteran said, 'You're right. Today you have been paid a full day's wages, but you are returning only half a day's work in exchange for them. You are being lazy. In other words, you are stealing half a loaf.' As an employee we need to be diligent and put in the effort that is worthy of the day's wage. No one else may see it, but the Lord sees and he wants us to be conscientious in all things.

A related and important lesson Proverbs teaches is that we are to save a little of what we earn and so be ready for the 'rainy day'. 'Go to the ant, O sluggard; consider her ways, and be wise. Without having any chief, officer, or ruler, she prepares her bread in summer and gathers her food in harvest' (6:6-8). The ant busies herself in the summertime, storing up food for the winter when there will be a shortage. We're called to be savers, yet without making the fatal mistake of thinking that our stockpiles are our ultimate source of security.

You Sluggard!

Proverbs introduces us to a character who is at once both tragic and funny: the sluggard. The sluggard is a person who is characterized by habitual laziness. 'How long will you lie there, O sluggard? When will you arise from your sleep? A little sleep, a little slumber, a little folding of the hands to rest, and poverty will come upon you like a robber, and want like an armed man' (6:9-11). Is Scripture advocating all work and no play? Is there anything wrong with rest and leisure and contemplation? Absolutely not! If we do not have those things in sufficient supply, then we are as unbalanced in our 'busyness' as the sluggard is in his laziness. But the person who can never get himself motivated to work lets life slip away by degrees.

Some of the biggest time wasters in our day are television, video games and the internet. All of them can be useful and fun, but they must be enjoyed in moderation. Minutes in front of the screen can so easily turn into hours, and hours into days. Eventually inertia takes over; nothing is accomplished, and so much time is lost. There's no way to recover time lost in this way. How easily life can be frittered away in such thoughtless unproductivity!

In the poem 'If', Rudyard Kipling wrote,

> If you can fill the unforgiving minute
> with sixty seconds worth of distance run,
> yours is the world, and everything that's in it.
> And what is more you'll be a man, my son.

Kipling is teaching us to focus on the minute and not to waste it; use your time wisely and apply yourself to the task in hand.

The accumulation of little things becomes great things. Proverbs tells us that the diligent ant has two particular characteristics that make her so noteworthy. First, she is self-motivated, a self-starter who does not need an officer or a ruler to tell her to get to work. Secondly, and more importantly, the ant is aware that time is slipping by. The summer is warm, food is abundant, yet she knows that as time passes, these days will end and hard times will come. So she takes advantage of the present and does not let the opportunity slip away. If we are self-starters and if we are conscious of time passing by, we will not be like the sluggard.

'The sluggard buries his hand in the dish and will not even bring it back to his mouth' (19:24). Here we see the good-for-nothing lazybones, lying half-starved; he reaches out his hand and puts it into the dish, and then before even bringing it back to his mouth, he thinks, 'I just need to rest for a few more minutes.' Can't we all be a little bit like the sluggard? Can't we also be like that in a spiritual sense? How easy it is for us to take all the good things the Lord provides and never to assimilate them, never to deploy them in doing the things the Lord wants us to be doing. Heed the warning: don't be a sluggard. Don't be lazy. 'The desire of the sluggard kills him, for his hands refuse to labour. All day long he craves and craves, but the righteous gives and does not hold back' (21:25-26). The sluggard refuses to work.

Laziness is a spiritual sin. In the church at Thessalonica a difficulty arose when some of the believers stopped work and withdrew from the world as they waited anxiously for the Lord Jesus to return. Presumably they expected the Lord to supply their needs in the meantime. Paul gave the church a very simple rule of thumb. 'If anyone is not willing to work, let him not eat' (2 Thess. 3:10). The sluggard likewise needs to be dealt with in such a straightforward fashion. 'I passed by the field of a sluggard, by the vineyard of a man lacking sense, and behold, it was all overgrown with thorns; the ground was covered with nettles, and its stone wall was broken down' (Prov. 24:30-31). Cathy and I used to share a spring garden with Ted and Cindy Melchers when we were newlyweds. It was easy to pull the weeds from the garden when they were small. It only took a bit of time and effort along the way. Sure, we had to break a sweat. We even had to swat a few mosquitoes, but such minor irritants are just part of life. Maintenance was easy, if done little and often. But if the weeds grew taller than the squash or okra, the task was soon overwhelming. How important it is then to learn the discipline of regularly maintaining all areas of one's life. How disheartening it must be to wake up one day only to discover that the walls are crumbling and the crops are overrun with weeds. A little diligence goes a long way.

Sometimes laziness arises from fear of the unknown. 'The sluggard says, "There is a lion in the road! There is a lion in the streets!" As a door turns on its hinges, so does a sluggard on his bed' (26:13-14). The sluggard thinks the world is a dangerous place; it's safer to stay in bed. He rolls over and goes back to sleep. Let us not succumb to fears, real or imaginary. Yes, there's risk; yes, there's pain; yes, it takes effort, but the Lord calls us to follow him in the way of diligence.

Live Generously

The book of Proverbs not only calls on us to work hard, to save for a rainy day, but it also calls us to be generous with our wealth. 'One gives freely, yet grows all the richer; another withholds what he should give, and only suffers want. Whoever brings blessing will be enriched, and one who waters will himself be watered' (11:24-25). We are not to be like the Dead Sea, forever receiving but never giving. Contrary to the wisdom of the world, the one who hoards will be found wanting one day. The one who gives generously will prosper. This is one of the great mysteries of God's providence.

Proverbs repeats this message several times. 'Whoever despises his neighbour is a sinner, but blessed is he who is generous to the poor' (14:21). It's easy to hoard our possessions, ignoring our neighbour who is in need. In reality it is the one who is generous who is going to prosper.

'Whoever is generous to the poor lends to the LORD, and he will repay him for his deed' (19:17). An act of charity to a poor person is really an act of charity to the Lord. Our Lord Jesus Christ taught that the one who gives a cup of water in his name to the least of his disciples will be rewarded for his kindness (*Matt.* 25:40). 'Whoever has a bountiful eye will be blessed, for he shares his bread with the poor' (22:9). And again, 'He who increases his wealth by interest and usury, gathers it for the one who is gracious to the poor' (28:8). The Lord is teaching us that he will bless those who are generous.

Is the Lord's blessing for our generosity a one-for-one correlation? In other words, does he match us dollar for dollar? No, the blessing may not be immediate and it may not be in the same coin. Nevertheless, his promise is sure. 'Whoever gives to the poor will not want, but he who hides his eyes will get many a curse' (28:27).

The New Testament picks up this theme. Paul writes in 2 Corinthians 9:6-7 about gathering a collection for the poor: 'whoever sows sparingly will also reap sparingly, and whoever sows bountifully will also reap bountifully. Each one must give as he has made up his mind, not reluctantly or under compulsion, for God loves a cheerful giver.' Jesus said in Luke 6:38: 'give, and it will be given to you. Good measure, pressed down, shaken together, running over, will be put into your lap. For with the measure you use it will be measured back to you.' We understand the illustration Jesus uses of people buying grain in the market. For a certain price the merchant would scoop out the grain and pour it into a container. And the Lord says in these verses, 'If you give generously, here's the measure by which I will give back to you. I will scoop up the grain. I will pack it down, I will shift it back and forth so that it settles nicely, and I will fill it again so that it comes up and over the top.' That's the measure by which the Lord will bless the one who is generous.

Ron Blue, founder of the financial planning services firm Ronald Blue & Co., says, 'I've spent a quarter-century studying financial and investment strategies . . . If I could boil down everything I have learned into one sentence or thought, it would be this: Generosity and financial freedom are inextricably linked.'[5] I had a good friend, Al Todd, who used to carry a $50 bill in his wallet for small emergencies. One day while eating at a restaurant, Al struck up a conversation with the waitress and learned of some difficulties she was experiencing. After the meal, Al quietly reached in his wallet and tucked the $50 under his coffee cup to tip the waitress. I'll never forget the sheer, inexplicable joy Al got out of helping a stranger. His explanation: 'She needs it worse than I do.'

One Christmas my father-in-law, Jim Edwards, learned that one of his young relatives wanted a new pair of waders for duck hunting. The young man's family couldn't afford such an extravagance. Jim went out and bought the waders, wrapped them, put them under the tree, and was absolutely bursting with excitement to present the gift on Christmas morning. Jim exemplifies the joy of generous living more than any other person I know. Fortunately, my daughter, Catharine, seems to be following in her grandfather's footsteps. Each Christmas or birthday I'm absolutely astounded by how carefully and thoughtfully she chooses the right gift for each person. She has found the secret of generosity: the giver gets the greatest joy and blessing.

Surely not Surety

Proverbs warns us not to become 'surety' for another. To be a surety for someone means to pledge our assets to repay their debts, such as co-signing a loan, guaranteeing a debt, or pledging assets to secure someone else's financial obligation. 'My son, if you have

---

[5] *Generous Living*, p.21 (Grand Rapids, MI: Zondervan Publishing House, 1997).

put up security for your neighbour, have given your pledge for a stranger, if you are snared in the words of your mouth, caught in the words of your mouth, then do this, my son, and save yourself, for you have come into the hand of your neighbour: go, hasten, and plead urgently with your neighbour. Give your eyes no sleep and your eyelids no slumber; save yourself like a gazelle from the hand of the hunter, like a bird from the hand of the fowler' (6:1-5). 'Whoever puts up security for a stranger will surely suffer harm, but he who hates striking hands in pledge is secure' (11:15). 'One who lacks sense gives a pledge and puts up security in the presence of his neighbour' (17:18).

What's wrong with becoming surety for someone else? The trouble is that we are presuming on the future. We are assuming that when the debt collector comes to our door we will have the cash available to satisfy him. 'Be not one of those who give pledges, who put up security for debts. If you have nothing with which to pay, why should your bed be taken from under you?' (22:26-27).

Making a gift to someone, of course, is entirely different from co-signing a loan for them. If I have the desire and the ability to help someone financially, then I should just go ahead and give it to them. But to enable them to borrow money without a known source of repayment or a proven track record of debt repayment courts disaster. Nothing but heartache will come from being a surety.

'Take a man's garment when he has put up security for a stranger, and hold it in pledge when he puts up security for foreigners' (20:16). In other words, if he's such a fool that he will co-sign for someone else, go ahead and have him sign into the debtors prison, because he's going to end up there eventually. You may have the money today, but when the debt is due to be paid you may not. Why take the risk?

The following is a true excerpt from a letter received by one of my clients:

Dear _____ :

Last year your son, John, came to me and asked that I co-sign a loan to help him get started in his new business. The bank required a second signature because as a start up business, John technically would have little or no income. With his house as collateral and because John was my best friend, I co-signed a note for $66,000 . . .

When things started to go bad for John, I implored him to pay his mortgage on time as my wife and I were mortified over the embarrassment of being dunned by a bank. John finally got so far behind that I agreed to step in and pay the interest myself so that they would not bring the property to foreclosure . . .

The only thing that could prevent me from losing the entire $66,000 plus interest is if the house sells for top dollar. Now the real estate market is bad and it looks like I will lose all the money. The bank that once supplied me with credit is now suing me. My credit and reputation have been destroyed. I don't have the money to pay the bank their $66,000 and things are going to get worse . . .

A few weeks ago my father died. It's ironic to me that the $60,000 that I will inherit from a lifetime of my father's efforts, his legacy to his son, will now be forfeited to your son . . .

Regards, _____

No more painful or true words can be found: 'The rich rules over the poor, and the borrower is the slave of the lender' (22:7).

Do Not Withhold Your Tithe

The final word on wealth is a reminder from Proverbs that all we have really belongs to the Lord. The scriptural principle of tithing—returning to the Lord a portion of what he has entrusted to us—is affirmed by Solomon. 'Honour the LORD with your wealth and with the first fruits of all your produce; then your barns will be filled with plenty, and your vats will be bursting with wine' (3:9-

10). The Lord makes it very clear throughout Scripture, from Genesis through to the epistles of the New Testament, that we are to acknowledge his lordship over us by honouring him with our wealth. Notice that the offering is to be from the 'first fruits'—it is to be taken off the top. It is to be set aside first, not taken from the leftovers, if and when our other expenses have been covered.

Cathy and I can testify to the Lord's faithfulness in meeting our needs, even when she was taking courses at the College of Charleston and I was earning a whopping $13,000 per year as an accountant in 1981. No matter the income, the barns have been filled with plenty and the vats with new wine.

We sometimes are tempted to think, 'I need a certain amount to live on, then when I get more comfortable I can begin tithing.' No, if we are faithful in small things then we will be faithful in larger things. 'Bring the full tithes into the storehouse, that there may be food in my house. And thereby put me to the test, says the LORD of hosts, if I will not open the windows of heaven for you and pour down for you a blessing until there is no more need' (*Mal.* 3:10).

Summary

The bottom line is simple: the Lord will honour those who honour him with their wealth. Whether it's in doing the right things like working honestly and diligently, sharing with others generously, or whether it's avoiding the pitfalls of trusting in one's riches or becoming surety for others, if we honour him with our material wealth, he will honour us with his blessing and grace. It's such a simple trade-off. Walk in his ways, and the Lord will be our shield and our reward will be very great (*Gen.* 17).

Key Principle: God honours those who honour him with their wealth.

Wisdom	Warnings
1. Hold material things lightly.	1. Don't trust in riches.
2. Be content.	2. Don't be anxious.
3. Be honest.	3. Don't cheat or steal.
4. Be diligent.	4. Don't be negligent or lazy.
5. Be generous and giving.	5. Don't take advantage of others (usury) or act as surety for another's debts.
6. Tithe.	6. Don't withhold from God.

3

FRIENDS AND NEIGHBOURS

'Friendship is the wine of life', said Samuel Johnson. Good friends not only add sweetness to our lives, but their positive influence is one of the keys to fruitful, abundant living.

The Hebrew word for 'friend' or 'associate' appears often in the book of Proverbs. In this book the Lord instructs the wise in the building of healthy relationships. This little Hebrew word for friend has many uses. It sometimes refers to an intimate friend or companion—someone who is in our inner circle. At other times it may refer to a neighbour, those who either live or work around us and with whom we have regular contact. Sometimes the word refers to a casual acquaintance, someone we know but not very well. Its precise meaning depends on the context in which it is used.

It is helpful to think of our relationships in concentric circles.

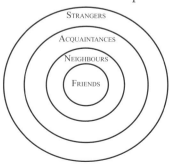

The small group of friends and companions at the centre is the most important—those relationships in which we invest the most time and energy. The second group, our neighbours, includes the people who live around us, co-workers and others whose day-to-day activities bring us in regular and close proximity.

Will You Be My Friend?

Let's start at the centre with our friends. Proverbs emphasizes the importance of carefully choosing the people with whom we spend most of our time.

When the Lord created the earth and put Adam in it, what was one of the first observations God made about his creation? 'It is not good that the man should be alone' (*Gen.* 2:18). Certainly this observation applies primarily to Adam's need for a complementary helper suitable to his needs. In grace the Lord created Eve and presented her to Adam before joining this first man and woman in holy matrimony. But the Lord's observation surely has a general application also. Human beings are not islands, and in every aspect of life we need the help and the encouragement of intimate friends. Not only will such friends keep us on the right track, but their good companionship will make life's journey more productive and enjoyable.

Scripture supplies us with some examples of intimate friendships. Jonathan and David were good friends who encouraged, helped, and protected one another (*1 Sam.* 18-20). Many years after Jonathan's death, David kept the vow of loyalty he had made with his friend by providing for the needs of Mephibosheth, Jonathan's crippled son, and treating him like one of his own family (*2 Sam.* 9). David's actions exemplify true covenant friendship.

Another example of intimate friendship is the relationship between the Lord Jesus and his 'beloved disciple' John. The apostle

John was by the Lord's side at each key stage in his public life and ministry. When Jesus stood on the Mount of Transfiguration, John was there with him. In the Upper Room at the Last Supper, John was the one reclining next to Jesus at the table. Theirs was a close and loving friendship, and it must have been one of the choicest blessings of the Lord's life on earth.

There are many others to whom we could refer—Elizabeth and Mary, Paul and Timothy, Ruth and Naomi. The essence of this kind of true companionship is summed up so well in Ruth's words to Naomi: 'For where you go I will go, and where you lodge I will lodge. Your people shall be my people, and your God my God' (*Ruth* 1:16).

By far the most important quality to look out for in those who would be your close friends is godliness—an integration of faith and character. The importance of choosing godly friends cannot be overstated. Proverbs puts this lesson in stark terms when it teaches us that we become just like the people with whom we spend most of our time. 'Whoever walks with the wise becomes wise, but the companion of fools will suffer harm' (*Prov.* 13:20). Again, 'Leave the presence of a fool, for there you do not meet words of knowledge' (14:7). Or even more bluntly, 'Make no friendship with a man given to anger, nor go with a wrathful man, lest you learn his ways and entangle yourself in a snare' (22:24-25). The words, attitudes, and values of our friends influence our thoughts and actions, and we will reflect the character of our friends—for better or for worse.

One of the concerns of political leaders within American society is the rapid rise in gang activity. Mayor Bob Coble, currently serving his third term as mayor of Columbia, South Carolina, spoke to a group of educators in December 2006. In his remarks, he said that gangs in the Columbia area, especially active in the high schools, represented the single greatest problem within our community. The territorial violence and related drug and other criminal activities, he said, have at their root a sense of social abandonment and a yearning for the sense of belonging. In other words, the attraction of gang membership for a young person is the feeling of companionship and the acceptance that comes from the other members of the group. The challenge facing parents and community leaders is the restoration of family and church to their rightful and essential roles in providing a loving, nurturing environment in which young people will feel love and acceptance.

> My son, if sinners entice you, do not consent. If they say, 'Come with us, let us lie in wait for blood; let us ambush the innocent without reason; like Sheol let us swallow them alive, and whole, like those who go down to the pit; we shall find all precious goods, we shall fill our houses with plunder; throw in your lot among us; we will all have one purse'—my son, do not walk in the way with them; hold back your foot from their paths, for their feet run to evil, and they make haste to shed blood. For in vain is a net spread in the sight of any bird, but these men lie in wait for their own blood; they set an ambush for their own lives' (1:10-18).

How do we develop godly friendships in our own lives, and in the lives of our young people? Proverbs teaches four essential principles of friendship: loyalty, candour, counsel and forbearance. To develop and keep close friends, and to profit mutually from the relationship, we must practise these four virtues.

Loyalty

The first virtue is loyalty. 'A friend loves at all times, and a brother is born for adversity' (17:17). 'Many a man proclaims his own steadfast love, but a faithful man who can find?' (20:6). 'Do not forsake your friend and your father's friend, and do not go to your brother's house in the day of your calamity. Better is a neighbour who is near than a brother who is far away' (27:10). A true friend sticks with us through thick and thin, and doesn't abandon us when we are down.

Proverbs warns us not to be a fair-weather friend. 'Many seek the favour of a generous man, and everyone is a friend to a man who gives gifts. All a poor man's brothers hate him; how much more do his friends go far from him! He pursues them with words, but does not have them' (19:6-7). It's easy to love someone when times are happy, and when things are going well. But what happens when that friend falls on hard times or falls by the wayside in his walk with the Lord? Are we going to be a fair weather friend who immediately turns our back and cuts that person off? We are called to a high degree of loyalty, yet without letting ourselves be dragged down.

We are also warned about spreading ourselves too thin, trying to be all things to all people. 'A man of many companions may come to ruin, but there is a friend who sticks closer than a brother. A man of many friends comes to ruin' (18:24). The person who is just a crowd-pleaser, who has a multitude of friends on a superficial level, never puts down deep roots in the good soil of godly companionship. Having a few godly friends is far better than having many shallow acquaintances. Our God is a covenant God. He promised thousands of years ago that he would never forsake his people throughout the generations. He stands by his promise. Likewise, we are called to be like the Lord and to be steadfast with our covenant friends. We are to love them, bless them, help them, always remain loyal to them. Loyalty is the chief characteristic of a friend.

In 1825, John Adams, the second president of the United States, was nearing the end of his long and successful life. He and Thomas Jefferson, his presidential successor and life-long acquaintance, frequently corresponded. They had weathered serious personal and political disagreements over the years, but they were eventually reconciled and their friendship was restored. In one of his final letters to Jefferson, Adams wrote,

> Every line from you exhilarates my spirits and gives me a glow of pleasure ... The little strength of mind and the considerable strength of body that I once possessed appear to be all gone, but while I breathe I shall be your friend.

In the end, relationships matter more than accomplishments.

Loyalty to a friend will occasionally require us to sacrifice other pursuits so that we can spend time together. The poet Robert Frost captured this concept in these words:

> When a friend calls to me from the road
> And slows his horse to a meaningful walk
> I don't stand still and look around
> On all the hills I haven't hoed
> And shout from where I am, "What is it?"
> No, now is a time to talk.
> I thrust my hoe in the mellow ground
> Blade end up, and I go up to the stone wall
> For a friendly visit.
>
> 'A Time To Talk'.

Candour

The second mark of true friendship is candour—openness and frankness in all that is said and done. A friend is not a friend who merely accepts us as we are, but one who truly wants us to improve, and who will guide us along the right path. 'Faithful are the wounds of a friend; profuse are the kisses of an enemy' (*Prov.* 27:6). 'Whoever rebukes a man will afterward find more favour than he who flatters with his tongue' (28:23).

A true friend is willing to confront us and candidly deal with attitudes or behaviour that we need to change. It may seem that a loving friend would overlook all our flaws and say only those things that we want to hear—'You are looking great; you are doing fine; do whatever it takes to make yourself happy.' But if they are not being sincere and truthful then the false encourager is no friend at all. 'A man who flatters his neighbour spreads a net for his feet' (29:5).

Nathan was bold in confronting King David about his adultery with Bathsheba—'You are the man!' (*2 Sam.* 12:7). Paul dealt openly with Peter's hypocrisy over eating 'unclean' food when alone with the Gentiles yet refraining from such food when his fellow Jews were present—'I opposed him to his face' (*Gal.* 2:11). Though no one likes to be confronted with one's faults and errors, tough love requires it. In Matthew 18:15 the Lord said: 'If your brother sins against you, go and tell him his fault, between you and him alone. If he listens to you, you have gained your brother.' A true friend is willing to be candid.

Counsel

The third quality of true friendship is counsel. Friends will bounce ideas off each other, share their plans and aspirations, and give each other their insight and wisdom. 'Oil and perfume make the heart glad, and the sweetness of a friend comes from his earnest counsel' (*Prov.* 27:9). The value of friendship goes far beyond having someone with whom to spend our leisure time. It is for this reason that godly friends are so important. Friendship should involve mutual improvement: 'Iron sharpens iron, and one man sharpens another' (27:17).

For no one is wise counsel more vital than those engaged in leadership: 'take away the wicked from the presence of the king, and his throne will be established in righteousness' (25:5). In other words, the advice a leader receives from his inner circle of friends sets the tone for key policies and decisions. Wise counsel leads to wise governance, whether corporate, governmental, religious or family: 'for by wise guidance you can wage your war, and in abundance of counsellors there is victory' (24:6). 'Without counsel plans fail, but with many advisers they succeed' (15:22). All leaders ought to consciously cultivate an inner circle of godly friends and companions on whom to rely. Often such relationships will be formed over the course of many years. For all of us, whether in leadership positions or not, there is wisdom in seeking advice before making key decisions. (See Chapter 8.)

Tact

Finally, an essential quality in a good friend is tact. *Random House Dictionary of the English Language* defines tact as 'a keen sense of what to do or say to avoid giving offence; skill in dealing with difficult situations.' This is what Proverbs calls wisdom in the way we treat our friends. For example, it's easy to overstay our welcome or to take advantage of friendship. 'Let your foot be seldom in your neighbour's house, lest he have his fill of you and hate you' (*Prov.* 25:17). Be careful not to abuse your relationship with your friends so that they begin to view you as a burden rather than a blessing.

Tact requires us to be careful not to be an irritant or a source of conflict. 'Whoever blesses his neighbour with a loud voice, rising early in the morning, will be counted as cursing' (27:14). 'Like a madman who throws firebrands, arrows, and death is the man who deceives his neighbour and says, "I am only joking!"' (26:18-19). I played high school football at Hammond Academy with a team mate who illustrated this principle. I was a lineman, he was a fullback, and in practice we had a blocking drill in which he was supposed to take the hand off and run to the right or left behind my block. Occasionally, just for fun, he would run neither right nor left. Instead, he would put his head down and drive his helmet right into the middle of my back. Then he would laugh and pick me up. I didn't think it was very funny. Actions speak louder than words, and a person who abuses a relationship, though calling himself a friend, is really a tactless irritant.

Proverbs also implores us to use tact in our speech. 'A dishonest man spreads strife, and a whisperer separates close friends' (16:28). 'Whoever covers an offence seeks love, but he who repeats a matter separates close friends' (17:9). We all do or say foolish things from time to time, and a good friend is willing to overlook our folly. A godly friend will forgive and forget, not keep the offence in the lower drawer to be pulled out and revisited on a recurring basis. Unconditional love, overlooking rather than remembering personal offences, is the way to build and maintain godly friendships.

The use of tact in all we say and do is illustrated in what Dr Glen Knecht, former senior pastor of First Presbyterian Church of Columbia, used to call the 'bucket principle'. In one hand, he would say, you hold a bucket of water and in the other hand a bucket of gasoline. When someone says or does something to start a little conflagration, you have the choice of which bucket to pour on the 'flames'. Choose the water, not the gasoline! The wise person extinguishes the fires of strife with tactful silence or soft words. The fool ignites a conflagration by repeating gossip or by making angry, harsh or groundless accusations.

Putting It All Together: Accountability

All of the hallmarks of true friendship—loyalty, candour, counsel and tact—are best captured in small accountability groups. Over the years I have met one-to-one with a number of dear friends—Ransey Bowers, Rick McCain, Will Haynie, Cubby Culbertson, Bill Jones, E. C. Burnett, George Murray, J. R. Murphy, Bill Bradshaw, and most recently, Gregory Hudgens—for Bible study, prayer, and accountability. We met periodically for a number of months or years, agreeing to be honest with one another about our personal walk with the Lord, our times of Bible study and private worship, and our relationships with our wives and families. These intimate friendships drive personal growth and spiritual maturity. The purpose and tone of such personal accountability is captured in what Paul wrote to his dear friends at the church in Philippi:

> And it is my prayer that your love may abound more and more, with knowledge and all discernment, so that you may approve what is excellent, and so be pure and blameless for the day of Christ, filled with the fruit of righteousness that comes through Jesus Christ, to the glory and praise of God (*Phil.* 1:9-11).

Howdy, Neighbour!

Moving outward from the circle of closest friends and companions, we come to our neighbours. These are those who live around us or with whom we work on a daily basis, yet who are one step removed from our inner circle. Whereas we only have a relatively few intimate friends, we typically have more neighbours and colleagues. How are we to treat them?

One of the key principles in dealing with neighbours is that we should live in peace with them as far as is possible.

There's something about living in close proximity to others that can cause irritation. We are all naturally prone to being critical, cynical, and easily irritated with our neighbours. Like a sore the irritation festers and grows. Over time it can erupt into open animosity or conflict, and our words and actions can so quickly spin out of control.

Proverbs warns against starting a conflict with our neighbour. 'Do not plan evil against your neighbour, who dwells trustingly beside you' (3:29). 'Nip it in the bud' is good advice. Neighbours are to be cherished, peace is to be preserved, goodwill is to be nurtured. Scripture warns us to not neglect or abuse the relationship, but to handle it gently, just we would a valuable piece of crystal. Heed the warning—'Fragile: Handle with care!'

Misunderstandings and disagreements with our neighbours may arise from time to time. We must manage the conflict, not perpetuate it, once it arises: 'What your eyes have seen do not hastily bring into court, for what will you do in the end, when your neighbour puts you to shame? Argue your case with your neighbour himself' (25:7-9).

Basic conflict management skills require us to: (1.) Overlook minor faults and offences; (2.) When truly offended, first examine one's own actions and attitudes for sin ('first take the log out of our own eye . . .', *Matt.* 7:5) (3.) Go directly to the offending party and openly discuss the problem, rather than talking to others; (4.) Listen carefully and understand the other party's perspective or explanation; (5.) Where possible, find creative solutions to solve problems or differences; and (6.) Be willing to forgive the offence and put the incident entirely behind you.

Many years ago a missionary arrived in a new country and settled into life in a rural area. His first task was to clear fields, dig ditches and build retaining ponds to capture rain for watering his crops (see *Prov.* 24:27). Immediately after completing the irrigation system, rain came and his neighbour, a stranger at the time, intentionally cut a breach in the ditch so that the missionary's water was diverted into the neighbour's fields. The missionary repaired the breach, didn't say anything, and then not long afterwards it happened again. Being mindful of his call to do everything in his power to stop the conflict, he went to his neighbour and offered to help build the man's irrigation ditches and banks. The shocked neighbour accepted his offer. The missionary found that by investing his time and energy in the wellbeing of his neighbour his own attitude toward that neighbour improved. In forsaking his anger he found a friend! Working with his neighbour transformed conflict into friendship.

In the New Testament, the Apostle Peter summarizes the standard for dealing with others. 'Do not repay evil for evil or reviling for reviling, but on the contrary, bless, for to this you were called, that you may obtain a blessing' (*2 Pet.* 3:9).

In 1981 a fire broke out in First Presbyterian Church of Columbia, rendering the sanctuary unusable. While the building was being renovated, the church across the street, Washington Street United Methodist, altered their schedule and allowed the Presbyterians to meet in their sanctuary on Sunday mornings for worship. Some years later, while I was serving on the Board of Deacons of First Presbyterian Church, a complaint was raised that our parking spaces were getting scarce because those Methodists across the street were parking in our parking lot and walking across the street for their services. 'What are we going to do about it?' That demand was met by the wisest response I have ever heard in a board meeting: 'I can tell you what we're going to do about it: Nothing! They did something very generous for us, and we are not going to return evil for good.'

How can we, who have been forgiven and blessed by our Heavenly Father, turn around and do evil to our fellow man? The Apostle John writes: 'If anyone says, "I love God", and hates his brother, he is a liar; for he who does not love his brother whom he has seen cannot love God whom he has not seen' (*1 John* 4:20).

In one of his parables, the Lord Jesus Christ told of a servant who had been forgiven a large debt by his master. The forgiven servant then found someone who owed him a small debt and immediately wanted to throw his debtor into jail for failing to pay his trifling debt. Likewise, how can we who have been forgiven so much and who have been given so many great blessings in the gospel, hold a grudge against the neighbour who has wronged us and not forgive? Proverbs 24:29 warns: 'Do not say, "I will do to him as he has done to me; I will pay the man back for what he has done."' Who gives us the authority to retaliate against our neighbour?

We are to be charitable in our thoughts and judgments as well as in our actions regarding our neighbour. 'Whoever belittles his neighbour lacks sense, but a man of understanding remains silent' (11:12). It is so easy to be critical. When a neighbour or colleague does something in a way that fails to meet with our approval, we are quick to say, 'What a fool!' Yet the one who belittles his neighbour like this is the one who lacks sense. We must learn to bite our tongues: 'Be not a witness against your neighbour without cause' (24:28).

In these principles of friendship taught in the book of Proverbs we hear echoes of the ninth commandment: 'You shall not bear false witness against your neighbour' (*Exod.* 20:16). It is our duty to maintain and promote the truth, and to do nothing prejudicial or injurious to our neighbour or his good name. The Apostle Paul summarizes our duty to our neighbour in this way: 'Love does no wrong to a neighbour; therefore love is the fulfilling of the law' (*Rom.* 13:10).

If my relationship with my neighbour is characterized first and foremost by love, then it will transform everything I do. If I am leaving my house for work in the morning and see that my neighbour's trash can has been knocked over and is spilling onto the street, then I will stop and pick it up. Why?—because I love my neighbour. Indeed, the whole way in which I will treat my neighbour, his possessions, his children, his wife will be dramatically altered by this principle of love.

Summary

The Lord has placed us in our neighbourhood, in our job, in our church. The people around us are our neighbours. Some of them will become our great friends. Some of them may turn out to be our enemies. Most will fall into that large middle category of acquaintances whom we will not know all that well. Yet if we handle each one of those relationships in the attitude of love, then we are living with our neighbours in a way that pleases the Lord. Our relationship with our neighbour is sacred.

Key Principle: We become like the people with whom we spend most of our time.

4

WORDS

Surprisingly there is more teaching in the book of Proverbs on the use of the tongue than on any other subject. About ninety separate proverbs warn us about the power of speech and instruct us on how best to control our tongues. But why is there such a sharp focus on mere words? The answer may astonish us: 'Death and life are in the power of the tongue, and those who love it will eat its fruits' (18:21). At first glance this may seem like a bit of an overstatement, but experience bears out the truth of these words. Things of great value and importance often come in small packages. Words may seem insignificant but they can pack a mighty punch!

Weapons of Crass Destruction

When we were children we often heard it said that 'Sticks and stones may break my bones, but words will never hurt me.' While repeating these lines in the heat of an argument may appear to make us impervious to ridicule or slander, they are simply not true. Words are powerful. The power to destroy others or to build them up lies on the tip of the tongue.

Words have the power to penetrate deeply into the human soul, whether for evil or for good. 'There is one whose rash words are like sword thrusts, but the tongue of the wise brings healing' (12:18). The writer compares an evil man's words to a person wielding a sharp sword. Like a sword thrust, words penetrate deeply and often leave the victim seriously wounded. The alarming thing is that we can so carelessly and recklessly inflict wounds on others without even realizing it.

One day at church I noticed one of the groundsmen sitting on a bench in the churchyard. Going over to chat, I observed a truly remarkable pencil drawing he was completing. 'Are you a trained artist?' I asked, perhaps with a note of surprise in my voice. 'No', he said sadly. 'When I was in first grade my teacher scolded me in front of the class, and said my drawings were childish and terrible. I was so embarrassed I never drew again until I was grown.' It was evident that the wound made forty or fifty years earlier was still being felt.

By contrast, a wise person will use words to heal. 'Anxiety in a man's heart weighs him down, but a good word makes him glad' (12:25). It is astonishing the effect positive words can have on those who hear them. An encouraging word can lift the spirit of a person who is weighed down with burdens and anxieties, making them feel so much better. 'Gracious words are like a honeycomb, sweetness to the soul and health to the body' (16:24).

Cast your mind back to the positive words others have said to you, and recall how they lifted your spirit. I remember receiving a thank-you letter, which was full of gratitude and praise for something I had done. I read that letter four times and deeply appreciated the words that someone had taken the time and effort to write. '[A] word in season, how good it is!' (15:23).

Aware of the impact our words can have, we must choose them so carefully. James says of the tongue, 'It is a restless evil, full of deadly poison' (*James* 3:8). He uses the metaphor of a snake which strikes by injecting its venom into its prey. The poison spreads quickly. Soon the flesh around the wound dies and rots, then sloughs away. Our words can be just as deadly.

How can words injure someone? Criticism, cursing, gossip and slander are different forms of destructive speech. Proverbs warns us about each one.

Criticism

According to Proverbs the 'scoffer' is the person who uses harsh or false words to tear others down, or to stir up conflict. 'A worthless man plots evil, and his speech is like a scorching fire' (16:27). 'A fool's lips walk into a fight, and his mouth invites a beating' (18:6). 'Drive out a scoffer, and strife will go out, and quarrelling and abuse will cease' (22:10). 'As charcoal to hot embers and wood to fire, so is a quarrelsome man for kindling strife' (26:21).

Cursing

Cursing and profanity come under the heading of 'perverse' speech in Proverbs. The spoken word was intended for conveying the truth. 'The mouth of the righteous is a fountain of life . . . On the lips of him who has understanding, wisdom is found' (10:11, 13). To use the tongue for cursing our neighbour is to pervert its noble use. 'A gentle tongue is a tree of life, but perverseness in it breaks the spirit' (15:4). 'A man . . . with a dishonest tongue falls into calamity' (17:20). 'Better is a poor person who walks in his integrity than one who is crooked in speech and is a fool' (19:1). 'If one curses his father or his mother, his lamp will be put out in utter darkness' (20:20).

Gossip

Gossip is the spreading of a rumour of a personal nature—usually one that is unflattering and unproven. Such chatty talk may seem to be innocent enough at times, but it is not. 'The words of a whisperer are like delicious morsels; they go down into the inner parts of the body' (18:8). The words we often whisper without much thought may have a deep and lasting impact on how the person concerned is viewed by others.

I recall a specific example of this in my business. I was talking to a woman in our office about another one of our employees, and in the course of the conversation she said: 'She and her husband have charged all their credit cards to the limit, and now they're having trouble making the payments.' Without even realizing it, my view of the employee in question was greatly diminished. How could she and her husband be so irresponsible? Here I was, her employer, and unknown to her, every time she passed me in the office I was thinking, 'You fool.' Words penetrate deeply into our consciousness and they alter the way we view other people. Because we can secretly destroy others with our words, Proverbs warns us bluntly: 'do not associate with a simple babbler' (20:19b). 'For lack of wood the fire goes out, and where there is no whisperer, quarrelling ceases' (26:20). Any church, business, family, or team that puts an end to gossip and instead fosters direct, honest communication will prosper.

Slander

Worse than gossip, however, is slander. Slander is an intentionally false statement, aimed at harming another's reputation. Slander is so destructive that even the strongest relationships can be undermined. 'A dishonest man spreads strife, and a whisperer separates close friends' (16:28). The slanderer is so dangerous a comparison could be drawn between him and a suicide bomber. He is so intent on destroying others he doesn't mind going down with them. 'Whoever utters slander is a fool' (10:18).

If words are so powerful, what guidance does Proverbs give us in knowing how and when to speak? By grace we can learn to filter our words, and the effort will be worthwhile. It all boils down to knowing the "facts."

Speak Only the F.A.C.T.S.

How are we to govern our speech? Proverbs teaches us to speak only the F.A.C.T.S.: our words should be Few, Apt, Calm, True, and Sweet.

Few

Compared to the constant stream of thoughts that race through our mind, our words should be few in number. 'Whoever restrains his words has knowledge, and he who has a cool spirit is a man of understanding' (17:27-28). This doesn't mean that we should never open our mouths. Rather, we all need to install a filter between our minds and our mouths, between our thoughts and our words. Sometimes it may be wiser to say nothing.

Back in my high school football days one of the coaches often quipped, 'It's better to keep your mouth shut and let others think you're a fool, than to open your mouth and remove all doubt.' That was his way of making the same point. When it comes to our words, less is more.

Some people simply talk too much. You know the type—they never stop talking long enough to take a breath. They are fearful of silence and must fill every quiet space with words. 'When words are many, transgression is not lacking' (10:19). If we talk incessantly, the opportunities multiply for a little bit of gossip, a little bit of cursing, a little bit of lying, a little bit of embellishment to pop out of our mouths. Something unhelpful, unedifying, unwholesome, or corrupt will slip out from between our teeth and so it is wise to let our words be few.

Certainly we are all different in the way we process our thoughts. Some people are extroverts; they think out loud. They say this and this and this ... and do not necessarily mean any of it until they get to the final statement. Others are introverts, who process thoughts inwardly before they speak. They think, but never say a word until they get to the end of their thought process. It is helpful in all of our relationships to be aware of how others process their thoughts. Generally, fewer words are better because 'When words are many, transgression is not lacking' (10:19).

'Whoever guards his mouth preserves his life; he who opens wide his lips comes to ruin' (13:3). The person who talks incessantly, even when there is nothing worth saying, tends towards ruin. One of my partners once refused to hire a well-qualified job applicant, noting that 'He loves to talk, and when he's talking, he sure isn't listening!'

Some people have the bad habit of giving the answer before the question has even been asked. 'The heart of the righteous ponders how to answer, but the mouth of the wicked pours out evil things' (15:28). 'If one gives an answer before he hears, it is his folly and shame' (18:13). 'Do you see a man who is hasty in his words? There is more hope for a fool than for him' (29:20). 'A fool takes no pleasure in understanding, but only in expressing his opinion' (18:2). We have to learn to hold our tongue until we are certain we understand the question. Jumping ahead in a conversation without first listening carefully and before formulating a measured response will cause many a misunderstanding. We do well to heed the words of James: 'Let every person be quick to hear, slow to speak, slow to anger' (*James* 1:19).

There is another reason why our words should be few. We should know when to bury a matter rather than to keep it alive by repeating it. 'Whoever goes about slandering reveals secrets, but he who is trustworthy in spirit keeps a thing covered' (11:13). What if we hear something that, even if it is true, should not be repeated? We must be able to keep a secret, to hold something in confidence, for the protection of the reputations of others.

When our son, Bryan, was about three years old, he could never keep a secret. One Christmas I bought a jar of special hand cream for the children to give their mother. Bryan and I wrapped the gift and placed it quietly under the tree while Cathy was in another room. As soon as she came in a few minutes later, he ran over to the package, pointed to it and said 'Dat's cream!' We can smile at his childish inability to keep a secret, but such an inability in those of more mature years is no laughing matter: 'Whoever keeps his mouth and his tongue keeps himself out of trouble' (21:23). We need to keep a close eye on our words for they can get us into trouble so very quickly.

Apt

Our speech must be appropriate, or 'apt'. Aptness means that our words must be direct and to the point. 'To make an apt answer is a joy to a man, and a word in season, how good it is!' (15:23). It is possible to say the right thing at the wrong time. That does little or no good. We can say the right thing in the wrong way, and that too does no good. The right word at the right time in the right way is healing to the bones. It is one of the marks of true wisdom.

Proverbs compares appropriate speech to the art work of a skilled craftsman. 'A word fitly spoken is like apples of gold in a setting of silver' (25:11). 'There is gold and abundance of costly stones, but the lips of knowledge are a precious jewel' (20:15). When we truly realize just what an impact our words can have, ought we not to choose words that will minister encouragement and spiritual health? Such words will change the way the hearer feels about himself. They will also change the way I feel about him, because I have chosen to be encouraging. And they will also change the attitude of those who might happen to learn of it or to overhear it.

Saying what is apt does not mean we are to falsely build up someone. In fact, such an approach is identified as 'flattery' in the book of Proverbs. Flattery is saying nice things either insincerely or inappropriately to another person's face. Dishonest compliments are no compliments at all. 'A lying tongue hates its victims, and a flattering mouth works ruin' (26:28). 'Whoever rebukes a man will afterward find more favour than he who flatters with his tongue' (28:23). 'A man who flatters his neighbour spreads a net for his feet' (29:5). The basic problem with flattery is it works. People believe the nice things they hear about themselves, even if they know they are not true!

Perhaps the greatest application of 'apt' speech is knowing when to confront or reprove someone else. If a friend needs to be reproved for inappropriate behaviour, then we must learn how to do it. 'Answer a fool according to his folly, lest he be wise in his own eyes' (26:5). 'Faithful are the wounds of a friend; profuse are the kisses of an enemy' (27:6). 'Whoever rebukes a man will afterward find more favour than he who flatters with his tongue' (28:23). The perfect example of a godly rebuke is found in 2 Samuel 12, when the prophet Nathan boldly confronted King David about his adultery with Bathsheba and his murder of her husband Uriah. The words, 'You are the man!' pierced David's heart like a spear, and though devastating, they led to the king's confession, repentance, and restoration. Tough love rebukes when necessary.

Calm

Angry words are rarely called for, and, if habitual, are a sign of a grave spiritual condition. Proverbs gives many strong warnings against angry words: 'A man of quick temper acts foolishly' (14:17). 'Whoever is slow to anger has great understanding, but he who has a hasty temper exalts folly' (14:29). 'Whoever is slow to anger is better than the mighty, and he who rules his spirit than he who takes a city' (16:32). 'Whoever restrains his words has knowledge, and he who has a cool spirit is a man of understanding' (17:27). 'It is an honour for a man to keep aloof from strife, but every fool will be quarrelling' (20:3). 'A fool gives full vent to his spirit, but a wise man quietly holds it back' (29:11). 'A man of wrath stirs up strife, and one given to anger causes much transgression' (29:22).

Some of us are more prone than others to fly into a rage, to lose our cool, to speak in a rash manner. Yet we cannot hide behind the excuse of our temperament. What other sins might I be predisposed to that don't need to be governed?

Why is it important to control our temper? Anger is the bitter root out of which the sin of murder grows. Jesus said,

> You have heard that it was said to those of old, 'You shall not murder; and whoever murders will be liable to judgment.' But I say to you that everyone who is angry with his brother will be liable to judgment; whoever insults his brother will be liable to the council; and whoever says, 'You fool!' will be liable to the hell of fire' (*Matt. 5:21-22*).

If we often find ourselves erupting in a volcanic explosion of harsh, angry words, we need to recognize our sin, confess it, and ask the Lord for grace to change. This is especially true if we are prone to cursing and profanity. Someone once said that profanity is the sign of a weak mind trying to express itself forcefully. More profound is the reason given in Proverbs to forsake anger: 'A soft answer turns away wrath, but a harsh word stirs up anger' (*Prov.* 15:1). By turning down the volume and carefully selecting our words we can stop controversy dead in its tracks. An angry response, on the other hand, merely stirs the hornets' nest. 'A hot-tempered man stirs up strife, but he who is slow to anger quiets contention' (15:18). 'The beginning of strife is like letting out water, so quit before the quarrel breaks out' (17:14). 'Scoffers set a city aflame, but the wise turn away wrath' (29:8). 'With patience a ruler may be persuaded, and a soft tongue will break a bone' (25:15).

True

The clearest message in Proverbs about the use of speech is that our words must be truthful and honest. 'Lying lips are an abomination to the LORD, but those who act faithfully are his delight' (12:22). 'There are six things that the LORD hates, seven that are an abomination to him: haughty eyes, a lying tongue, and hands that shed innocent blood, a heart that devises wicked plans, feet that make haste to run to evil, a false witness who breathes out lies, and one who sows discord among brothers' (6:16-19). 'The getting of treasures by a lying tongue is a fleeting vapour and a snare of death' (21:6). The world teaches us to say whatever we want in the pursuit of selfish gain. In other words, the end justifies the means. Proverbs says the world's way is foolish. If we have to be dishonest in order to get rich, then we are far better off going without, for wealth gained dishonestly leads to death.

The Lord so detests liars that he actively works against them. 'Truthful lips endure forever, but a lying tongue is but for a moment' (12:19). 'A false witness will not go unpunished, and he who breathes out lies will not escape' (19:5). 'A false witness will not go unpunished, and he who breathes out lies will perish' (19:9).

'A false witness will perish, but the word of a man who hears will endure' (21:28).

There is something profoundly noble about a person who earns a reputation for honesty. 'Righteous lips are the delight of a king, and he loves him who speaks what is right' (16:13). 'Whoever gives an honest answer kisses the lips' (24:26). To 'speak what is right' means to speak in a straightforward fashion. Leaders do not need to surround themselves with 'yes' men but rather with people who will speak the truth at all times and in every situation.

Likewise, a true friend is someone who will not hide the truth. 'Faithful are the wounds of a friend; profuse are the kisses of an enemy' (27:6). If there is something that needs to be addressed with my friend, I must be honest in addressing it with him. If I ignore it or stay silent about it, I am being dishonest with him. Straight speech means speaking the truth. The loving thing to do is to deal with problems when they arise.

Sweet

The ideal picture presented by Proverbs is a person whose speech is consistently encouraging, straightforward, and pure. Paul wrote to the Colossians, 'Let your speech always be gracious, seasoned with salt, so that you may know how you ought to answer each person' (*Col.* 4:6). 'Gracious words are like a honeycomb, sweetness to the soul and health to the body' (16:24). 'He who loves purity of heart, and whose speech is gracious, will have the king as his friend' (22:11).

Summary

'Death and life are in the power of the tongue' (*Prov.* 18:21). Positive, honest, truthful words are full of life and power for 'the tongue of the wise brings healing' (12:18). On the other hand, harmful, destructive, false words are full of the power of death, for 'A fool's mouth is his ruin, and his lips are a snare to his soul' (18:5). What we say reflects what is in our hearts and on our minds. 'The mouth of the righteous is a fountain of life . . . On the lips of him who has understanding, wisdom is found' (10:11, 13). Train your mind to focus on kind and helpful thoughts. Train your tongue to say only what is true, helpful and necessary. Look for opportunities to say something that will do good to those who will hear it, and see what happens. You never know what life-enhancing power will be in your words.

Key Principle: Speak only the F.A.C.T.S.—Let your words be Few, Apt, Calm, True, and Sweet.

5

SEXUAL PURITY

It was a struggle to decide on the final wording of the title to this chapter, because 'sexual purity' sounds so, well, 'puritanical'. And yet purity is just the right word—purity as in refreshing, satisfying, fulfilling. The message of Proverbs about sex is very simple: sex is a great blessing within the bounds of a loving marriage.

Essential to an understanding of Proverbs' teaching about sex is the basic biblical truth that God created mankind male and female. God created Adam and Eve for each other so that they would not be alone; they were to cleave to one another and become one flesh (*Gen.* 2:18, 24). The goal of marriage is oneness.

The physical and spiritual oneness of husband and wife is also intended to be a reflection of the oneness that exists in the Holy Trinity—the unity of the Father, Son and Holy Spirit: 'Let us make man in our image, after our likeness ... So God created man in his own image, in the image of God he created him; male and female he created them' (*Gen.* 1:26-27). Paul expounds on this theme when he writes to the Ephesians: 'In the same way husbands should love their wives as their own bodies. He who loves his wife loves himself. For no one ever hated his own flesh, but nourishes and cherishes it, just as Christ does the church' (*Eph.* 5:28-29).

Because of this very real spiritual dimension, sex is not a mere physical act. It involves body, mind and spirit. Some in the ancient world tried to deny this, just as many do in our modern world: 'This is the way of an adulteress: she eats and wipes her mouth and says, "I have done no wrong."' (*Prov.* 30:20). But pretending that extra-marital sex is just a physical act, and no more wrong than having lunch and a glass of water, is a perversion of one of the most precious gifts God has bestowed on mankind. The life experience of many has proved that sexual purity is a source of blessing and joy; sexual promiscuity is a source of emptiness and sorrow.

Though Proverbs has more to say about speech than any other subject, sexual purity comes a close second. The majority of chapters 5 through 7 is devoted to a warning against sexual immorality and an encouragement to staying faithful to one's spouse. The moral principles of God's creation are clear: sexual relations are reserved exclusively for the life-long companionship of one man and one woman within the marriage covenant.

Don't Get Burned

Many of the proverbs in this book emphasize the stark contrast between the rewards of faithfulness and the consequences of unfaithfulness. On the one hand, they teach that sexual purity is a spring of life. On the other hand, they warn that sexual sin destroys the soul. The contrast is not between a negative and a neutral. The contrast is between a negative and a very strong positive; between great pain on the one hand and great blessing on the other.

The warnings given are blunt, since the law of sexual faithfulness is as simple and as absolute as the law of gravity. There are no exceptions.

Keep your way far from her, and do not go near the door of her house, lest you give your honour to others and your years to the merciless, lest strangers take their fill of your strength, and your labours go to the house of a foreigner, and at the end of your life you groan, when your flesh and body are consumed and you say, 'How I hated discipline, and my heart despised reproof!' (5:8-11).

At our farm, Limerick, we have an outdoor fire pit we call the 'council fire'. It's a circular brick structure, perfect for a roaring fire and evening conversation. When our kids were young we had to enforce an absolute rule: no walking on the bricks! Invariably, the morning after the logs seemed to have burned out, a child would walk on the bricks, stumble into the smouldering embers, and get burned. It happens every time, without fail—if you step in the embers, you get burned. So it is with sexual dalliances.

> Can a man carry fire next to his chest and his clothes not be burned? Or can one walk on hot coals and his feet not be scorched? So is he who goes in to his neighbour's wife; none who touches her will go unpunished. People do not despise a thief if he steals to satisfy his appetite when he is hungry, but if he is caught, he will pay sevenfold; he will give all the goods of his house. He who commits adultery lacks sense; he who does it destroys himself. Wounds and dishonour will he get, and his disgrace will not be wiped away. (6:27-33).

Speaking to the naïve, the book of Proverbs underscores the inevitable and dire consequences of casual, extra-marital sex.

> I have seen among the simple, I have perceived among the youths, a young man lacking sense, passing along the street near her corner, taking the road to her house in the twilight, in the evening, at the time of night and darkness. And behold, the woman meets him, dressed as a prostitute, wily of heart . . . With much seductive speech she persuades him; with her smooth talk she compels him. All at once he follows her, as an ox goes to the slaughter, or as a stag is caught fast till an arrow pierces its liver; as a bird rushes into a snare; he does not know that it will cost him his life. (7:7-23).

Why are the warnings so dire? Because sexual sin destroys the life and soul of those who breach the marriage covenant. Notice that each warning speaks in terms of life and death; 'for wisdom will come into your heart, and knowledge will be pleasant to your soul . . . So you will be delivered from the forbidden woman, from the adulteress with her smooth words, who forsakes the companion of her youth and forgets the covenant of her God; for her house sinks down to death, and her paths to the departed; none who go to her come back, nor do they regain the paths of life' (2:10, 16-19). 'For the lips of a forbidden woman drip honey, and her speech is smoother than oil, but in the end she is bitter as wormwood, sharp as a two-edged sword. Her feet go down to death; her steps follow the path to Sheol; she does not ponder the path of life' (5:3-6). 'For . . . the adulteress . . . hunts down a precious life.' (6:23-26). 'For . . . the . . . young man lacking sense . . . does not know that it will cost him his life' (7:6, 23). 'Her house is the way to Sheol, going down to the chambers of death' (7:27). 'But he does not know that the dead are there, that her guests are in the depths of Sheol' (9:18). For the ancient Hebrews, Sheol was the grave, the place of the dead. But it also had a darker, more fearful aspect, that of hell itself. 'The path of life leads upward for the prudent, that he may turn away from Sheol [i.e., hell] beneath' (15:24).

The physical consequences of sexual sin are also far-reaching. They range from the inconvenient (STDs or sexually transmitted diseases, which may or may not be treatable), to the life-changing (unplanned pregnancies), to the life-ending (AIDS, cervical cancer, abortion, etc.). The impact on legitimate relationships, though less tangible, can be just as severe: guilt, anger, alienation, loss of trust, inability to achieve intimacy and sexual harmony with one's spouse, and divorce.

Notice that the names given to the seductress in Proverbs vary: 'the forbidden woman' (2:16; 5:3, 20; 22:14); 'the adulteress' (2:16;

5:20; 6:24; 7:5; 23:27; 27:13; 30:20); 'the woman Folly' (9:13); 'the evil woman' (6:24); 'prostitute' (6:26; 7:10; 23:27; 29:3). Each of these titles suggests that only one's husband or wife is a natural and fulfilling sexual partner. Sex is reserved exclusively for marriage, and the oneness of covenant love can only be achieved inside that special bond. The sacred oneness in marriage is destroyed when sex takes place with a third person.

Intimate sexual relations with a stranger, though perhaps enticing, can never satisfy. God made us in such a way that we can only find sexual fulfilment and satisfaction within the exclusive relationship of marriage. The pleasure of an extra-marital affair is at best only fleeting and it is inexorably followed by misery and sorrow. 'For the lips of a forbidden woman drip honey, and her speech is smoother than oil, but in the end she is bitter as wormwood, sharp as a two-edged sword. Her feet go down to death; her steps follow the path to Sheol; she does not ponder the path of life; her ways wander, and she does not know it' (5:3-5). 'The woman Folly is loud; she is seductive and knows nothing . . . And to him who lacks sense she says, "Stolen water is sweet, and bread eaten in secret is pleasant." But he does not know that the dead are there, that her guests are in the depths of Sheol' (9:13, 18). 'The mouth of forbidden women is a deep pit; he with whom the LORD is angry will fall into it' (22:14). 'For a prostitute is a deep pit; an adulteress is a narrow well' (23:27). Paul clearly articulated this same principle when he wrote, 'Or do you not know that he who is joined to a prostitute becomes one body with her? For, as it is written, "The two will become one flesh." . . . Flee from sexual immorality. Every other sin a person commits is outside the body, but the sexually immoral person sins against his own body' (*1 Cor.* 6:16, 18).

The seventh commandment simply states, 'You shall not commit adultery' (*Exod.* 20:14). The Hebrew word for adultery literally means illicit intercourse, or sexual activity outside of marriage.

God felt so strongly that his people should refrain from such sin that the Old Testament law provided one universal penalty for adultery—death (*Lev.* 20:10).

Though now the civil and ceremonial aspects of the Old Testament law have been abrogated by Christ, he made it clear that the moral commands of God's law remain intact. He came not to abolish but to fulfil the law (*Matt.* 5:17). Therefore not only the eternal but also the temporal consequences of the law remain as absolute as ever. Are the warnings of Proverbs an exaggeration or are they a reflection of reality? Have you and I not seen many situations in which lives have been shattered and ruined as a result of adultery?

I have a friend whose early days were full of family happiness. His relationship with his dad was as close as that of any father and son. They did things together, went to sports activities together, they had a fabulous relationship. The father was clearly the centre of the boy's universe. Then, tragically, the father had an affair with a woman at his work, and soon decided to leave his wife and family in order to live with her. Besides destroying his wife's life, his actions devastated the little boy. This little lad was no longer the apple of his father's eye; he was now an outcast—forgotten and tossed aside. His self-worth was shot to pieces. From being a model child he turned into a problem student overnight. He became rebellious, angry and recklessly self-destructive. He became sexually active in his early teens and his girlfriend fell pregnant. She was a professing Christian, but he talked her into having an abortion. Clearly, here was a series of bad choices by several individuals, but there was unquestionably a spill-over effect. It began in the life of the father, poured over into the life of the wife, then into the son, then into the girlfriend, then into the aborted child, and then into future spouses and generations to come. The pain and destruction was a consequence of one man who chose the fleeting pleasure of an illicit affair. 'Like a bird that strays from its nest is a man who strays from his home' (27:8). In other words, he acts just like a mother hen who abandons her nest, and leaves her eggs to be ruined by the elements or destroyed by predators.

The sexual drive that stirs within is natural. Kept in check, it is a positive, natural force compelling a young person to search for a spouse. But allowed to run unchecked, it leads to deviant behaviour and destructive habits. Not the least of these is pornography—written words and visual images portraying graphic sexual activity. Pornography fuels the fire of lust, especially for men who are more visually stimulated sexually than women. What we see and read we think about. What we think about we do. 'Let your eyes look directly forward, and your gaze be straight before you. Ponder the path of your feet; then all your ways will be sure' (4:25-26).

Pornography has been a problem for centuries, but through the Internet it is now sweeping across the world. From the 'tame' to the most abandoned forms of sexual perversion, the unlimited and inexpensive access to such mind-boggling vulgarity is destroying lives and marriages on a colossal scale. The disturbing thing about pornography is that it fuels rather than satisfies the desire for sexual gratification. It makes the sexually frustrated worse rather than better! It builds higher levels of sexual tension and distraction, which is relieved only by self-gratification or by sexual activity with others, in an insane pattern of ever diminishing pleasure alongside ever increasing addiction. How true the observation: 'Sheol and Abaddon are never satisfied, and never satisfied are the eyes of man' (27:20).

How can a person, whether married or single, avoid the destructive snare of pornography?

Firstly, by asking the Lord for grace to exercise self-control (see chapter 6).

Secondly, by memorizing Scripture so that it can be recalled and used effectively as the 'sword of the Spirit' the very moment when sexual frustration and temptation arise. 'How can a young man keep his way pure? By guarding it according to your word. With my whole heart I seek you; let me not wander from your commandments! I have stored up your word in my heart, that I might not sin against you' (*Psa.* 119: 9-11).

Thirdly, by having one or more close friends with whom you can meet at set times for the express purpose of sharing intimate details about one's spiritual walk. In my own experience I have found this sense of accountability an invaluable way to plant a hedge around my own world. Have you ever thought about giving a close and trusted friend access to your computer passwords to check websites visited, or arranging to call each other from a hotel room or airport when away from home to report success or failure in bookstores visited or television programmes viewed, etc? 'Iron sharpens iron, and one man sharpens another' (27:17). The point is to guard one another's back, just as Jonathan and David made a covenant to protect and care for one another as brothers for life (*1 Sam.* 18:3).

Blessings on Blessings

If a person is not married, sexual purity involves chastity—abstinence from sexual relations. If a person is married, sexual purity involves fidelity—forsaking of all others and cleaving only to one's spouse. The goal of such companionship is not to limit but rather to enhance mutual pleasure and satisfaction.

I am strongly convinced that the 'Thou shall nots' are aimed at preserving and enhancing our pleasure through a lifetime of commitment. God is no cosmic kill-joy who attempts to squelch our sensual feelings. He simply knows that such passions can only be sustained and positively directed within marriage. He is the one who created us male and female, gave the command to be fruitful and multiply, and then stood back and said, 'This is all very good." (*Gen.* 1:27-31). He delights in what he has made, including sexual relations between husband and wife.

> Drink water from your own cistern, flowing water from your own well. Should your springs be scattered abroad, streams of water in the streets? Let them be for yourself alone, and not for strangers with you. Let your fountain be blessed, and rejoice in the wife of your youth, a lovely deer, a graceful doe. Let her breasts fill you at all times with delight; be intoxicated always in her love. Why should you be intoxicated, my son, with a forbidden woman and embrace the bosom of an adulteress? (*Prov.* 5:15-20).

The marriage relationship is to be guarded and nurtured. 'Keep your heart with all vigilance, for from it flow the springs of life' (4:23). The water from a fresh spring is not only satisfying, but is constantly replenished. An illicit sexual encounter may satisfy for a few fleeting seconds, but its thrill is only temporary and cannot be sustained. Sex within marriage alone is both refreshing and renewable. God has provided a life-long source of exquisite pleasure. The poet John Milton, in *Paradise Lost,* calls wedded love a 'perpetual fountain of domestic sweets'.

This is one of many aspects of life in which the Puritans like Milton have so much to teach us, for they really got it right. As explained by Leland Ryken[1], sex within marriage was not only legitimate in the Puritan view, but it was meant to be exhilarating. William Gouge, a Puritan pastor, said that 'married couples should engage in sex with good will and delight, willingly, readily, and cheerfully'. An anonymous Puritan wrote that 'when two are made one by marriage, they may joyfully give due benevolence, one to the other, as two musical instruments rightly fitted do make a most pleas-

---

[1] Leland Ryken, *Worldly Saints: The Puritans As They Really Were* (Grand Rapids, MI: Zondervan, 1986).

ant and sweet harmony in a well-tuned consort.' Another, Alexander Nicole, said that 'in marriage, thou not only unitest thyself unto a friend for comfort and society but also a companion for pleasure.' The Puritans rejected the mistaken notion that sexual love within marriage was anything less than a divine blessing. In their view God had given the entire physical world, including sexual relations within marriage, for the wellbeing of mankind.

God's approval of married love is seen in the book of Proverbs, particularly in its admiration for the wonders of the natural world: 'Three things are too wonderful for me; four I do not understand: the way of an eagle in the sky, the way of a serpent on a rock, the way of a ship on the high seas, and the way of a man with a virgin' (30:18-19). The same palpable wonder was expressed by Solomon in his chronicle of sexual love between a bridegroom and his beautiful bride: 'Eat, friends, drink, and be drunk with love!' (*Song of Sol.* 5:1).

The fences God provides for our life (e.g. 'You shall not commit adultery') are not to keep us out of green pastures, but to keep us in green pastures. At Limerick, we once had two goats, Bucky and Job. One was an Alpine, the other a Nubian, but they both had the same innate goat tendency: the grass always seemed greener on the other side. Even in the richest pasture, they would get on their front knees and strain their necks through the fence, trying desperately to nibble the weeds just beyond their reach. How much like those goats we are! Our divine shepherd has provided lush pastures, free of the pests and dangers that lurk on the other side of the fence, for our wellbeing and enjoyment. Stay at home and graze to your heart's content.

Lessons in Love

The application of Proverbs to attaining and sustaining a fulfilling marital relationship can be summarized in these lessons:

1. Do all in your power to uphold all marriages—your own and the marriages of others.

This begins with the obvious—refrain from extra-marital relations—but it extends to maintaining purity in speech (no sexual jokes, sexual innuendo, or flirtatious conversation) and purity in conduct (no overly friendly physical contact with members of the opposite sex, no travelling together or spending extended periods together in private without safeguards and accountability). Pray for the protection of your marriage and others'. Always let your spouse know your whereabouts, and let him or her have unfettered access to you by phone without a secretary screening your calls. Openness and accountability foster trust, which in turns generates intimacy with one's spouse.

2. God intends us to have one spouse for life—wait for the one!

Make the commitment to be a one-woman man or a one-man woman. For the unmarried, this will mean waiting for the one, exclusive relationship that God has ordained for you. For the married this will mean living gratefully within the one, exclusive relationship that God has ordained for you.

3. Renew your physical love for your spouse.

Any relationship can grow stale or cold through neglect. Taking time to tend the garden will keep it fresh and in good shape.

Remember too that oneness is not the same thing as sameness. Cathy's parents, Jim and Ann Edwards, have long sung the virtues of an occasional 'naughty weekend' (romantic getaway) to keep life interesting. Do what you reasonably can to observe 'date nights', to periodically get away from home, the kids and the office, and to have sufficient privacy at home and while on vacation. Be proactive in staying fit and healthy, and maintain good personal hygiene.

4. Talk to your children openly and honestly about sex—spell out the warnings as well as the blessings.

We have tried to teach our children the facts of life so that they would not be victims of ignorance or misinformation. Giving our children a healthy sense of their sexual identity and an appreciation for the mystery of God's divine blessing on married love provides a solid foundation for a lifetime of satisfaction. During one evening's newscast, in which the danger of AIDs was reported, nine-year old Miriam asked Cathy how does one get AIDs. Cathy replied it could be through taking intravenous drugs with contaminated needles, or through having sex with a person who had many sexual partners. Miriam then asked, 'But what if you marry someone who's been married before?' Whereupon four-year old Catharine, who had been listening silently to the conversation, weighed in and said, 'I'd just take him to the hospital and have him tested!' All of life is a teaching opportunity. Six-year old Bryan, after a successful deer hunt at the farm, asked me, 'Why was that buck running across the field? Was he looking for sex?' Before I could do more than nod, Bryan walked away with a satisfied grin on his face. That was all he needed to know at the time.

5. *God forgives and restores past failures.*

We are all capable of making very bad decisions in life. From the snare of pornography, to the guilt of premarital sex, to the destructiveness of an extramarital affair, the Lord is merciful and kind: 'As a father shows compassion to his children, so the LORD shows compassion to those who fear him. For he knows our frame; he remembers that we are dust' (*Psa.* 103:13-14). 'Whoever conceals his transgressions will not prosper, but he who confesses and forsakes them will obtain mercy' (28:13). Let us be swift in seeking forgiveness. And remember, the Lord not only forgives but he also gives grace to overcome the temptations which so easily ensnare us. Be transparent in the accounts you give to your trusted fellow believers, to guard against repeated failures. 'So you will walk in the way of the good and keep to the paths of the righteous' (2:20).

Key Principle: Sexual sin destroys the soul, but sexual purity is a spring of life.

6

WORK

In the beginning God created work. The mandate given to Adam and Eve at their creation was, 'Be fruitful and multiply and fill the earth and subdue it and have dominion over the fish of the sea and over the birds of the heavens and over every living thing that moves on the earth' (*Gen.* 1:28). I believe God intended work to be both productive and rewarding, but something significant happened after Adam's fall: 'Cursed is the ground because of you; in pain you shall eat of it all the days of your life; thorns and thistles it shall bring forth for you; and you shall eat the plants of the field. By the sweat of your face you shall eat bread, till you return to the ground, for out of it you were taken; for you are dust, and to dust you shall return' (*Gen.* 3:17-19). Therefore, we now face a certain amount of opposition and frustration in doing the very thing we were called to do.

Yet if Christ came to destroy the works of the devil (*1 John* 3:8), surely one of his most significant acts was to restore work to a place of proper significance in the life of believers. Trained as a carpenter in Joseph's household, Jesus elevated all lawful human trades and endeavours. Jesus gave significance to our efforts to provide for ourselves and our families, to help meet the needs of others, and to labour for the common good of mankind.

Proverbs, not surprisingly, has a great deal to say about the daily occupations of mankind. Generally, it is not *what* we do but *how* we do it that matters the most.

Diligence

By far the dominant lesson of Proverbs is that we must be diligent in all our labour. Here is but a small sample of the many sayings on this important subject:

• 'A slack hand causes poverty, but the hand of the diligent makes rich. He who gathers in summer is a prudent son, but he who sleeps in harvest is a son who brings shame' (10:4-5).

• 'Whoever works his land will have plenty of bread, but he who follows worthless pursuits lacks sense' (12:11). Only the empty-headed keep their faces to the sky, daydreaming of easier chores and pleasurable recreation. The diligent keep their heads down, put their hands to the plough, and keep going. They will have plenty to eat.

• 'The hand of the diligent will rule, while the slothful will be put to forced labour' (12:24). The diligent will become the masters, the lazy the servants.

• 'The soul of the sluggard craves and gets nothing, while the soul of the diligent is richly supplied' (13:4).

• 'Whoever loves pleasure will be a poor man; he who loves wine and oil will not be rich' (21:17). If the love of recreation and rich cuisine dominate our waking hours, there will be no time for the diligence needed to succeed.

• 'I passed by the field of a sluggard, by the vineyard of a man lacking sense, and behold, it was all overgrown with thorns; the ground was covered with nettles, and its stone wall was broken down. Then I saw and considered it; I looked and received instruction. A little sleep, a little slumber, a little folding of the hands to rest, and poverty will come upon you like a robber, and want like an armed man' (24:30-34). It's interesting that weeds grow somewhat slowly and are easily pulled up when they are small. Over time the small job gets bigger and bigger, until it is completely beyond control. A little regular effort is far better than waiting a few more days until I'm better rested.

• 'She rises while it is yet night and provides food for her household and portions for her maidens. She considers a field and buys it; with the fruit of her hands she plants a vineyard. She dresses herself with strength and makes her arms strong. She perceives that her merchandise is profitable. Her lamp does not go out at night' (31:15-18). The diligence described in these verses does not come naturally; it must be learned. The virtues of being a good employee and developing work stamina—the brute determination to complete the job—are among life's most important skills.

The opposite of diligence is negligence, and Proverbs introduces us to two pathetic characters who have it in abundance: the Sloth and the Sluggard.

• 'Whoever is slothful will not roast his game, but the diligent man will get precious wealth' (12:27). In other words, the sloth is too lazy to gather fire wood even to prepare his own meals.

• 'The way of a sluggard is like a hedge of thorns, but the path of the upright is a level highway' (15:19). In other words, 'there is an element of dishonesty in laziness (trying to sidestep the facts and one's share of the load)' and 'the straight course is ultimately the easiest.' (Kidner, p. 115). Often the negligent spend more time and effort avoiding the job than the diligent spend completing the job!

• 'Slothfulness casts into a deep sleep, and an idle person will suffer hunger' (19:15).

• 'The sluggard buries his hand in the dish and will not even bring it back to his mouth' (19:24).

• 'Love not sleep, lest you come to poverty; open your eyes, and you will have plenty of bread' (20:13).

• 'The desire of the sluggard kills him, for his hands refuse to labour. All day long he craves and craves, but the righteous gives and does not hold back' (21:25-26). Though the sluggard wants, he refuses to put out effort to get.

• 'The sluggard says, "There is a lion outside! I shall be killed in the streets!"' (22:13). Some form of hysteria, fear, hypochondria, or sensationalism seems to grip these folks, and they never seem to get life in gear.

• 'As a door turns on its hinges, so does a sluggard on his bed' (26:14). Some folks so adore—and need!—sleep that they become permanently attached to the bed, like a door fixed to its hinges.

• 'Whoever works his land will have plenty of bread, but he who follows worthless pursuits will have plenty of poverty' (28:19). A special category of recognition goes to the daydreamer. Whether too creative or too good to do the mundane work of ploughing, he dreams of better ways of doing things. At the end of the day, he finds his cupboard is bare. He missed the story of *The Tortoise and the Hare* in kindergarten.

Master Craftsman

The call to diligence is more than a call to work until the whistle blows. Though a steady effort is important, there is a higher call to excellence. 'Do you see a man skilful in his work? He will stand before kings; he will not stand before obscure men' (22:29). This by no means teaches that we should be workaholics, sacrificing life's priorities on the altar of making either loads of money or a name for ourselves. Instead, what it teaches is that doing a few things well is better than doing many things poorly. A humble job done well is far better than a high-flying job done poorly.

Many Christian students have applied to my law firm over the years for various types of employment—file clerk, law clerk, or new attorney. A cursory review of their résumé sometimes reveals very marginal academic performance. Do they lack ability, or are they just lazy? Either answer may give cause for concern, but more so the latter. Behind all the excuses is the stark fact that they have just failed to apply themselves. Christian people are called to give of their very best. I have told my children that failure due to lack of effort is unacceptable.

Proverbs also teaches us to genuinely put our best foot forward—not as a hypocrite would do, pretending to be something he is not, but doing our best and being on our best behaviour because we belong to the Lord. On a certain highway in South

Carolina sits a large junkyard, with a massive 'Jesus is Lord!' sign hanging on the fence. The image always strikes me as incongruous. You may differ with me on this one, but it strikes me as putting a religious wrapper on a broken down, rusted collection of cast-offs. Like a perfectly healthy and able-bodied tramp begging for change while wearing a WWJD (What Would Jesus Do?) bracelet to curry favour and sympathy. I do not mean to cast aspersions on honest purveyors of second-hand equipment, but the point I want to make is that we are called to put forth our very best. The virtuous wife in Proverbs 31 is extolled because 'She looks well to the ways of her household and does not eat the bread of idleness' (31:27). The farmer and shepherd is admonished to 'Know well the condition of your flocks, and give attention to your herds . . . the lambs will provide your clothing, and the goats the price of a field. There will be enough goats' milk for your food, for the food of your household and maintenance for your girls' (27:23, 26-27). Extra diligence, extra skill will be rewarded.

Slacker!

I remember sitting in my dormitory room at Clemson University at the end of my freshman year, studying for my final accounting exam. I had been pulled in all sorts of directions that semester—intramural softball, Campus Crusade for Christ leadership team, visiting Cathy thirty miles away at Furman University—and I was not ready for this exam! During my devotional time one morning, I came across a verse in Proverbs that hit me like a brick: 'Whoever is slack in his work is a brother to him who destroys' (18:9). Guilty as charged! We are to do our work, as Paul says, as though we are working for Christ (*Eph.* 6:7). Not half-hearted. Not as men-pleasers and clock-watchers, simply trying to get by with the least amount of effort.

A recent phenomenon in the work place is the distraction of Internet sites and social networking services, which are accessible by computer during work hours. Facebook, MySpace, and E-Harmony (and thousands of other sports, news, political, and special-interest websites) are the modern vehicles for wasting large quantities of time. The following statement appeared in a recent article in *The State* newspaper, describing the MySpace website: 'Can you hear that loud sucking sound? It's the noise time makes when hours disappear at work with nothing to show for it but eye strain and MySpace overload.'[1] When we are on the job, we are to give 100% effort, not the minimum we can get away with. Clock-watchers, lunch-stretchers, and time-wasters are a brother to him who destroys. You might as well go to the copy room and start tearing up the equipment. You are already having a negative impact on your company.

First Things First

Proverbs warns us to plan our steps, prioritize the tasks, and tackle the most important thing first. 'The plans of the diligent lead surely to abundance, but everyone who is hasty comes only to poverty' (21:5). In other words, the wise person develops a game plan, a plan of attack, before tackling the job. Such plans lead to advantage, whereas the person who jumps in hastily without thinking things through will create waste and frustration. 'Prepare your work outside; get everything ready for yourself in the field, and after that build your house' (24:27). Though we may be tempted to do the comfortable thing first, like build a house, it is more critical to get the fields ploughed and planted so that there will be a harvest before the winter arrives. This is the way of nature: 'Go to the ant, O sluggard; consider her ways, and be wise. Without having

---

[1] 'Lost in MySpace and Liking It', *The State,* July 20, 2006.

any chief, officer, or ruler, she prepares her bread in summer and gathers her food in harvest.' (6:6-8).

It is often said that the good is the enemy of the best, and the urgent stands in the way of the important. Jesus was the master of sticking to his God-ordained agenda without being sidetracked by other demands on his time. Once, when the multitudes were searching for him in the hope of seeing him perform more miracles, the disciples tracked him down in the wilderness where he was praying alone. They urged him to return to town, but he said, 'Let us go on to the next towns, that I may preach there also, for that is why I came out' (*Mark* 2:38). We are likewise to live and work with a clear set of priorities.

Part of prioritizing is to plan ahead in life. We are to be savers without being hoarders. 'The sluggard does not plough in the autumn; he will seek at harvest and have nothing' (20:4). Other examples of wisely planning ahead are seen in nature: 'the ants are a people not strong, yet they provide their food in the summer' (30:24-26). There is a fine balance between wisely planning ahead and selfishly hoarding resources which could be better deployed in God's kingdom. Building bigger barns (or renting more and more storage units) may be a sign of not trusting God to take care of us. Maintaining the balance is critical. The ultimate question is, 'What is my motive?' Am I saving for a rainy day or trying to take God out of the equation by becoming self-sufficient? 'Do not toil to acquire wealth; be discerning enough to desist. When your eyes light on it, it is gone, for suddenly it sprouts wings, flying like an eagle toward heaven' (23:4-5). The Lord may test us from time to time, to see where our hope lies. He may test us with abundance, to see if we forget him; or he may test us with poverty, to see if we continue to bless his name and seek his favour. We are to trust the giver, not the gift.

Pay the Up-Front Price

Glen Knecht used to say, 'Pay the up-front price.' He meant we are to make the initial investment of time and effort early in the process, to obtain maximum results. This applies to our spiritual life (walking with the Lord and learning his ways in our youth) as well as to our world of work. Proverbs expounds the wisdom of this approach: 'Where there are no oxen, the manger is clean, but abundant crops come by the strength of the ox' (14:4). Every job can be done the right way or the 'just-enough-to-get-by' way. It's invariably worth the effort to marshal the resources—mentally and in other ways—to get off on the right foot. 'In all toil there is profit, but mere talk tends only to poverty' (14:23). Quit talking, roll up your sleeves, and get started.

Many implications flow from this approach. When I graduated from Clemson, one of my dormitory mates graduated with a degree in mechanical engineering. He got a high-paying job with a large international company, but was bitterly disillusioned after a few weeks at work. 'All they have me doing is sweeping floors and moving furniture', he complained to an older man, looking for sympathy. Instead of sympathy, he received a stern rebuke. 'Are you too good to move furniture? Move that furniture better than anybody has ever moved furniture before, and eventually they'll figure out you can handle responsibility!' In other words, shut up and do your job. Getting a little ox manure on the boots never hurt anybody.

Guilt by Association

The people we choose to work with—if we have a choice—determine the environment in which we will thrive or suffer. Call it the culture of the work place. Proverbs warns us to be careful in selecting our employees and work partners.

• 'My son, if sinners entice you, do not consent. If they say, "Come with us, let us lie in wait for blood" . . . my son, do not walk in the way with them; hold back your foot from their paths' (*Prov.* 1:10-15). The company we keep largely determines our destiny, because we become like the people with whom we spend most of our time. Their habits and ways become our habits and ways, for better or for worse.

• 'Like vinegar to the teeth and smoke to the eyes, so is the sluggard to those who send him' (10:26). Hiring a lazy person will be as painful to the employer as a blast of smoke in the eyes, and as unpleasant as a big swig of vinegar. I could add a number of real-life examples here, but even changing the names would not protect the guilty!

• 'A worker's appetite works for him; his mouth urges him on' (16:26). We have learned over the years at our law firm that hiring people who are 'hungry'—having a family to care for, a house to pay for, etc.—brings great focus and energy. The satiated, self-sufficient worker is usually far less diligent. Dr James Dobson of *Focus on the Family* once called the circumstances of a man who has a wife, children, and home to care for 'the straight life'; not meaning straight in sexual terms but in terms of industry and diligence. The hungry worker walks a straight path.

• 'Like an archer who wounds everyone is one who hires a passing fool or drunkard' (26:10). The employer who thoughtlessly hires just anybody to do the job will suffer for it. Like a 'loose cannon on the deck' the misfit worker will carelessly shoot in every direction. The character of those we hire is the single most important thing they bring to the work place. Most people can learn new job skills but a new character is practically impossible to get.

• 'The partner of a thief hates his own life; he hears the curse, but discloses nothing' (29:24). In other words, the innocent partner becomes a thief by complicity. He will be called to make good, or else become a thief by his own silence. Neither option is desirable.

Smell the Roses

A subtle but important lesson lies in the admonition to stop and smell the roses along the way. Proverbs tells us that the 'virtuous wife' has learned this delightful secret. 'She seeks wool and flax, and works with willing hands . . . She perceives that her merchandise is profitable. Her lamp does not go out at night . . . Strength and dignity are her clothing, and she laughs at the time to come' (31:13, 18, 25). Her work, though difficult, produces a sense of satisfaction. She takes delight in doing her job well. Taking a moment every now and then to pause and reflect on what has been accomplished so far is a great encouragement to keep pressing on.

When Bryan was about twelve years old, he and his 'partner', John Schooler, started a lawn service (*Two Boys and A Mower*). I told him to always stop after completing the mowing, weed-eating and leaf-blowing, and admire the 'end product'. Doing so produces a great sense of satisfaction (and greatly impresses the homeowner, if they see you 'enjoying' the fruit of one's labours). Any job worth doing is worth doing well and then admiring. Incidentally, there is a strong precedent for this in Genesis: 'And God saw everything that he had made, and behold, it was very good' (*Gen.* 1: 31).

Summary

Success in completing a job is almost guaranteed when we plan ahead, prioritize our steps, assemble the right team, make the upfront investment of time and resources, and diligently chip away at the task until it is finished. Sounds easy, doesn't it? Countless stories could illustrate the wisdom of gaining ground inch by inch. Dr Abraham Kuyper, Prime Minister of The Netherlands at the beginning of the twentieth century, was a politician, pastor, seminary president and professor, newspaper editor, and author. And he did several of these jobs simultaneously for decades! He was a master at using his time profitably and chipping away at the job in hand.

But my favourite illustration of this principle is my own maternal grandmother, Kate Davis Shealy, who died at the age of 87. 'Grandmother Kate' lived alone until she was 86, and single-handedly maintained a one-acre yard—mowing, raking, and weeding her way through each season. She would tackle a small patch of ground each day and then rest. By the time she got around the whole yard it was time to start over. But it was always beautiful. And so was her spirit.

Key Principles: All lawful employments honour the Lord and dignify man.

No job, done diligently and for the genuine service of God and others, will go unnoticed.

Success is faithfully doing to completion whatever God has called me to do.

7

SELF-CONTROL

When our children were small, a popular Bible song for kids taught them that 'Self-control is just controlling yourself.' Sometimes it is not that simple, is it? From childish behaviour—like throwing a temper tantrum or gorging on cookies before dinner—to adult problems—like anger, lust, drunkenness, gluttony, and addiction—trying to control our appetites and passions is a major challenge.

The main thrust of the teaching of Proverbs about self-control is that the spirit must rule over the body—we cannot let our physical appetites and passions run wild. 'A man without self-control is like a city broken into and left without walls' (25:28). Ancient cities were walled around to keep their inhabitants safe from pillaging enemies. If a city had great gaps in its defensive walls it would be easy prey for the enemy. Metaphorically, the person who lacks self-control is like that defenceless city.

Esau is the classic biblical example of someone who lacked self-control. Esau was a man who was ruled by his passions. One day he came home from hunting, and he was absolutely famished. His twin brother Jacob was cooking stew and offered Esau a bowlful on condition that Esau would give Jacob his birthright as the firstborn son. Esau replied, 'I am about to die; of what use is a birthright to me?' (*Gen.* 25:32). Thus Esau traded his inheritance for a bowl of stew! He displayed the same recklessness in taking wives for himself from among the cursed Canaanite people and in his hot-tempered intention to kill Jacob for stealing his father's blessing. Esau was a godless and immoral man (*Heb.* 12:16), who was impulsive, profane, and lacking in self-control.

As we saw in Chapter 4, we must exercise self-control over our words and emotions. Proverbs teaches us the importance of controlling our tongue and refraining from gossip, profanity, and expressions of anger. We must not allow our emotions to rule over us and influence our conduct towards others. This will be achieved primarily through guarding our thoughts and emotions with all diligence. 'Whoever restrains his words (i.e., exercises self-control) has knowledge, and he who has a cool spirit is a man of understanding' (17:27). Anger, bitterness, resentment and self-pity all have a self-focus which is sinful and destructive. Let them go!

Likewise, we saw in Chapter 5 the admonition to exercise self-control over our sexual desires. Christ taught in the Sermon on the Mount that we are not merely to refrain from adultery, but we are to exercise self-control over our thoughts (*Matt.* 5:27-30). The person who lacks self-control, when tempted with sexual sin, may dwell on the possibilities presented and in his mind indulge in a little 'harmless' day-dreaming. Such thoughts are the seeds which grow into the outward acts of fornication and adultery. It is best not to allow such seeds to be planted in the mind.

Now, obviously not every fit of anger leads to murder, and not every lustful thought leads to adultery. The point is that sin can be a slippery slope. One minute we think we are standing on solid ground, the next moment we have fallen headlong into the mire. Sin is not to be played with. Charles Spurgeon, the renowned preacher of Victorian London, understood this well when he wrote, 'He who eats the grapes of Sodom will drink the wine of Gomorrah.'[1]

One area of life that we have not yet examined is food and drink. Proverbs warns us that we also need to exercise self-control over our physical appetite. In fact, the enjoyment of daily food and drink is one of life's most basic pleasures. How do we enjoy the gift God has given us without over-indulging and having too much of a good thing?

Who's in Charge Here?

God created us to enjoy sensuous pleasures, but man's corrupted nature has reversed the order of things, and the pursuit of pleasure can so easily master us. That is why self-control is necessary: we are at war with our own sinful desires. Peter said, 'Beloved, I urge you as sojourners and exiles to abstain from the passions of the flesh, which wage war against your soul' (*1 Pet.* 2:11). Paul admonished believers to 'to put off your old self, which belongs to your former manner of life and is corrupt through deceitful desires' (*Eph.* 4:22). James echoed this thought when he said, 'each person is tempted when he is lured and enticed by his own desire' (*James* 1:14). Each of the apostles then reminded their readers about letting our natural tendencies toward anger, lust and lawlessness dominate us. Passions out of control destroy relationships, both with the Lord and with man, and that is exactly what Satan seeks to accomplish. Rebuilding the defensive wall torn down by sin is the goal of self-control.

---

[1] *Morning and Evening*, August 29.

Sow a Thought, Reap an Action

What is self-control, and where can we get it? The New Testament uses a word in Greek which is translated as temperance or self-control in our English versions. Self-control is the exercise of power or strength to control one's inner passions and cravings. When Paul lists self-control among the nine-fold fruit of the Spirit, he teaches us the important truth that self-control is a God-given 'grace' (*Gal.* 5:23). Or as he says to the Philippians, God works in us 'both to will and to work for his good pleasure' (*Phil.* 2:13).

Right behaviour springs from right thinking. 'To know wisdom and instruction, to understand words of insight . . . to receive instruction in wise dealing . . . to give prudence to the simple . . . Hear, my son, your father's instruction, and forsake not your mother's teaching' (1:2-4, 8). Essential to the exercise of self-control is the knowledge of what to do in life's many circumstances, understanding what are the best choices to make. We cannot live up to the standard if we do not know what the standard is. Scripture is a lamp to our feet and a light to our path (*Psa.* 119:105): it shows us what is the best path to follow.

Right behaviour is not achieved without the exercise of inner strength to follow what we know is the right path. With the Lord's help, supplying us with the grace we need, we can do this: 'If you turn at my reproof, behold, I will pour out my spirit to you; I will make my words known to you . . . Then you will understand righteousness and justice and equity, every good path; for wisdom will come into your heart, and knowledge will be pleasant to your soul; discretion will watch over you, understanding will guard you, delivering you from the way of evil, from men of perverted speech, who forsake the paths of uprightness to walk in the ways of darkness' (1:23; 2:9-13). Our heavenly Father supplies us with his Spirit to enable us to be obedient to him; and that obedience is sweet to the soul of every child of God, for 'his commands are not burdensome' (*1 John* 5:3).

I started driving a school bus for Hammond Academy when I was fifteen years old. (Fifteen! That would never happen in today's litigation-prone world.) To bar drivers from exceeding the speed limit, each bus in the fleet was equipped with a 'governor', a device on the engine that prevented the vehicle from exceeding a certain speed. The governor moderated the speed very effectively—the bus could never go over 50 miles per hour. Scripture, applied to our hearts and minds by the Holy Spirit, is like a governor on our life. It reins us in, keeping us under control. The combination of knowing what to do and having the Holy Spirit as our Comforter (Strengthener) will enable us to bring ourselves under control.

Experience teaches us that time spent reading Scripture, in prayerful dependence upon the Holy Spirit, provides the help we need to overcome our personal battles with passion and lust. Paul challenges believers to walk in newness of life when he writes: 'We know that our old self was crucified with him in order that the body of sin might be brought to nothing, so that we would no longer be enslaved to sin. For one who has died has been set free from sin . . . Let not sin therefore reign in your mortal bodies, to make you obey their passions' (*Rom.* 6: 6-7; 12).

> O to grace how great a debtor
> Daily I'm constrained to be!

The High Life or the Dull Life?

The familiar advertising slogan for Miller Beer captures well what we all want: *the high life!* ('You only go around once, so grab all the gusto you can get!'). In other words, we all want to live life to the full. The very idea of self-control may seem to imply that we are settling for second best. Yet Proverbs teaches us that, ironically, the satisfaction of our physical appetites comes from moderation, not from excess. We can call this the irony of pleasure: the more we have of it, the less it satisfies. Pursuing pleasure as an end in itself leads only to diminishing returns and hopeless frustration. Enjoyed in moderation, the ordinary pleasures of life are quite exquisite.

Who wants to live a dull and colourless life? Surely no one. There is great beauty, meaning and pleasure to be drawn from life (*Gen.* 1:28-31). In fact, Proverbs adds breathtaking insight into God's design for human existence. Wisdom, speaking as an eyewitness to creation, says: 'When he established the heavens, I was there . . . rejoicing in his inhabited world and delighting in the children of man' (*Prov.* 8:27, 31). Just as high-definition television is far superior to the old black and white television sets, and just as live music is much more rich and enjoyable than an AM radio broadcast, God's original design of the created world was for man's rich enjoyment. It was created to be vibrant, crisp, and delightful to the senses. But sin has taken away our HD TV's and replaced them with black and white sets. All creation groans under the curse of sin (*Gen.* 3:17-19; *Rom.* 8:20-22).

The Lord does not deny us earthly pleasures, but on the contrary he encourages those which are legitimate. The proper use of God's gifts (food, drink, sleep, recreation, sex) actually heightens rather than diminishes the sense of pleasure and satisfaction. The life of faith sweetens legitimate pleasures because it pursues them in harmony with sanctified reason and conscience. Jonathan Edwards, the great American preacher of the eighteenth century, taught that the wicked person enjoys illicit pleasure only while at war with himself, with fear rather than with the blessings of God. Having misappropriated the Lord's blessings by perverting them for sinful uses, the foolish find that the very pleasure they long for eludes them.

Fearfully and Wonderfully Made

God has created us body and soul. Though our physical and spiritual parts are distinct, they nevertheless have an impact on each other. What we do with our body affects our soul. What we do with our soul affects our body.

For example, I have found that consistent physical exercise has a direct impact not only on my body, but on my emotional and spiritual condition. The positive effects of exercise to limit stress, give energy, and curb the appetite, also noticeably improve my spiritual walk. Less stress reduces anger. More energy increases quality time with my family. Reduced appetite encourages moderation at the table. And so on.

It is important not to overstate the benefits of physical exercise. Paul wrote to Timothy, 'train yourself for godliness; for while bodily training is of some value, godliness is of value in every way, as it holds promise for the present life and also for the life to come' (*1 Tim.* 4:7-8). While I know that my mortal body will wear out and not last forever, my personal experience has been that both physical and spiritual disciplines are beneficial, and improve the quality of life in both the short and long term.

The human body is an incredibly complex and durable creation. Among other things, it is designed to experience exquisite pleasure. 'My son, eat honey, for it is good, and the drippings of the honeycomb are sweet to your taste' (*Prov.* 24:13). But it is also designed to react if we overindulge and get too much of a good thing. 'If you have found honey, eat only enough for you, lest you have your fill of it and vomit it' (25:16). 'It is not good to eat much honey' (25:27a). When I was a freshman at university, I woke up one Sunday without time for my normal breakfast before church. My room mate, Tommy Price, kept a large jar of honey in our room, so I ate three or four heaping tablespoons and headed out the door. I walked about half a block and that load of sugar hit me like a ton of bricks. The nausea was so severe I turned and made a dash for the dormitory. Lesson learned! And that pales in comparison to my one and only experience of chewing tobacco!

Now, honey may not be your weakness, but I imagine for most of us there is some food that we find hard to resist. For Cathy, it is chocolate. For my father-in-law, it is vanilla ice cream. For me, it is barbecue—I can literally eat it until I get sick, wait a short while, and then go back for more! But the warning of Proverbs is clear: eat only what you need.

Not only is too much food a bad thing for our bodies, it can be a bad thing for our soul too. Agur, one of the writers of Proverbs, prayed, 'feed me with the food that is needful for me, lest I be full and deny you and say, "Who is the LORD?"' (30:8-9). He understood that a consistently full belly can be like an anaesthesia for the soul. Somehow when we have an abundance of food and possessions we begin to think we have provided everything for ourselves, and we stop looking to God's hand for his provision of our needs.

Aside from the spiritual benefit of remembering where our food comes from, there is another practical benefit to moderation: 'A worker's appetite works for him; his mouth urges him on' (16:26). It is good to walk away from a meal feeling as if we could eat a little bit more, for that will spur us on. Eating to the point of being satiated is going too far.

An interesting benefit of self-control in what we eat is that moderation enhances the pleasure. 'One who is full loathes honey, but to one who is hungry everything bitter is sweet' (27:7). Learning to enjoy a moderate amount of food, and relishing each mouthful, rather than greedily eating beyond the point of satisfaction is important. Eat to live, don't live to eat!

Proverbs also warns us to be careful about the circumstances in which we dine, lest we dig a hole for ourselves with every spoonful. The aspiring social climber[2] is warned to eat moderately when dining with rulers and socialites. 'When you sit down to eat with a ruler, observe carefully what is before you, and put a knife to your throat if you are given to appetite. Do not desire his delicacies, for they are deceptive food' (23:1-3). And again, 'Do not eat the bread of a man who is stingy; do not desire his delicacies, for he is like one who is inwardly calculating. "Eat and drink!" he says to you, but his heart is not with you. You will vomit up the morsels that you have eaten, and waste your pleasant words' (23:6-8). In other words, do not let your appetite for fine food and powerful company cloud your judgment or leave you in their social debt. On more than one occasion, when dining with elected officials or leaders in business and political circles, I have witnessed the power of fine food and generous libations to lower the barriers of discretion. Eat before you go, and sip the wine, if at all, slowly!

Red, Red Wine

Let us spend a little bit more time thinking about alcohol. The important thing to remember about alcohol, compared to other types of food or drink, is that it has the power to assume control over us. In a progression which first impairs the senses and then takes over the thought process itself, alcohol alters the personality and suppresses the judgment. Intoxication is, by definition, the opposite of self-control!

That is why Proverbs is so blunt: 'Wine is a mocker, strong drink a brawler, and whoever is led astray by it is not wise' (20:1). The

---

[2] Kidner, p. 151.

wise person, being skilled at making life's best choices, quickly realizes the foolishness of intoxication. The way we react to the world is based on what we perceive. Alcohol, by dulling the senses and then ultimately taking over our judgment, interferes with our God-given ability to perceive and react to our surroundings.

Proverbs gives us a punch-list of troubles that go with alcohol abuse.

> Who has woe? Who has sorrow? Who has strife? Who has complaining? Who has wounds without cause? Who has redness of eyes? Those who tarry long over wine; those who go to try mixed wine. Do not look at wine when it is red, when it sparkles in the cup and goes down smoothly. In the end it bites like a serpent and stings like an adder. Your eyes will see strange things, and your heart utter perverse things. You will be like one who lies down in the midst of the sea, like one who lies on the top of a mast. 'They struck me', you will say, 'but I was not hurt; they beat me, but I did not feel it. When shall I awake? I must have another drink' (23:29-35).

In other words, those who overindulge in the consumption of alcohol put themselves in a position where unwanted harm will come upon them.

In human experience, we sometimes find that the Lord protects us in our folly. Sometimes the drunk will wake up the next morning still safely atop of the beam, or still breathing after the car has wrapped itself around a tree. But sometimes he does not. The failure to exercise self-control is a tempting of providence and an invitation to disaster in the life of every person. O for the grace of self-control!

For some, changing the company we keep may be a key to breaking the cycle of alcohol abuse. 'Be not among drunkards or among gluttonous eaters of meat, for the drunkard and the glutton will come to poverty, and slumber will clothe them with rags' (23:20-21). As stated in Chapter 3, we become like the people with whom we spend most of our time. Keeping company with the sober may yield great benefits in terms of self-control.

My law partner, Bill Sweeny, gives a personal testimony to the power of the Lord to break an addiction to alcohol. When Bill was in his early 40s, and not a believer in Jesus Christ, he had quite a reputation for heavy bouts of drinking and reckless behaviour. Dating back to his college fraternity days and his years in the Navy, Bill was on the path to self-destruction. When he trusted in Christ, his entire world was turned upside down. The first thing to go was the taste for alcohol—without asking or realizing it, he no longer craved the escape it once offered. Because he no longer drank heavily, his golf buddies and the old crowd of friends began to fall away—Bill wasn't as much 'fun' as he used to be. One thing led to another, and within a few months he was graciously and gloriously delivered from self-destruction to newness of life.

Summary

What steps can we follow in the pursuit of self-control?

1. Know your weaknesses!

Each of us struggles with various and perhaps differing problems, and we have to be self-aware to know where we are particularly prone to temptation and sin. 'The prudent sees danger and hides himself, but the simple go on and suffer for it' (27:12). A political consultant I know uses the following admonition: 'If you want to hunt ducks, you have to go where the ducks are.' The spiritual corollary is, 'If you want to avoid sin, don't go to the place of temptation.'

2. Draw on both the promises and warnings of Scripture and store them up in your heart daily.

Wisdom says, 'Blessed is the one who listens to me, watching daily at my gates, waiting beside my doors' (8:34).

3. Ask the Lord for the grace of self-control.

'Whoever is simple, let him turn in here! To him who lacks sense she says, "Come, eat of my bread and drink of the wine I have mixed. Leave your simple ways, and live, and walk in the way of insight"' (9:4-6).

4. Pray for our nation.

The common belief that each person can behave in any way he wants, so long as it doesn't harm others, completely misses the mark. How we live affects others. 'Righteousness exalts a nation, but sin is a reproach to any people' (14:34). The character of the nation consists of millions of individual choices. The last stanza of 'God Bless America' ends with the prayer that God will 'mend thine every flaw; confirm thy soul in self-control, thy liberty in law.'

Key Principle: Self-control is the grace of inner strength, enabling us to do, say and think that which pleases God. Our spirit must rule over our body.

8

GUIDANCE

One November morning before dawn I was at the farm, preparing for a deer hunt. I had set out my hunting gear the night before—gun, coat, boots, gloves, binoculars, etc.—but could not find my flashlight. 'No problem', I thought to myself when leaving the house. 'I can find the stand—I know this place like the back of my hand.' But I had not counted on thick clouds obscuring the moon and stars. It was so dark I could not see my hand in front of my face. I stumbled and meandered my way past the Scuppernong vineyard, through the fields, and ended up—in the wrong place! When the morning began to dawn, I could follow my tracks and see clearly where I had left the path.

The Lord has not left his children in the dark to stumble along the path of life. What help does God give us for the journey? His promise to guide us: 'Trust in the LORD with all your heart, and do not lean on your own understanding. In all your ways acknowledge him, and he will make straight your paths' (3:5-6). We must give up something ('our own understanding'—the natural way we do things) and take on something ('trust the Lord'—obey his directions).

The greatest challenge in the believer's life is learning to walk by faith and not by sight.

A Lamp to My Feet

The tangible benefit of having a light in the darkness is obvious: knowing where to walk. Not only knowing which path to take, but also avoiding the potholes and stumbling blocks that might lie in the path. The Lord has given us a bright lantern in the form of his word:

• 'I have taught you the way of wisdom; I have led you in the paths of uprightness. When you walk, your step will not be hampered, and if you run, you will not stumble. Keep hold of instruction; do not let go; guard her, for she is your life' (4:11-13).

• 'When you walk, they will lead you; when you lie down, they will watch over you; and when you awake, they will talk with you. For the commandment is a lamp and the teaching a light, and the reproofs of discipline are the way of life' (6:22-23).

• 'Whoever despises the word brings destruction on himself, but he who reveres the commandment will be rewarded' (13:13).

• 'Whoever gives thought to the word will discover good, and blessed is he who trusts in the LORD' (16:20).

• 'Whoever keeps the commandment keeps his life; he who despises his ways will die' (19:16).

Dr John MacArthur recounts a chilling tale in his book, *The Vanishing Conscience*.[1] An Avianca Airlines jet crashed in the mountains of Spain in 1986, killing all the passengers and crew aboard. When the flight recorder was recovered from the scene, the investigators learned what had happened. Shortly before the crash, an automatic warning system alarm sounded: 'Pull up! Pull up!' But the pilot, thinking it was mistaken, said, 'Shut up!' and switched it off. He thought he knew his location and flight path better than the plane's computer. In the same way, Scripture is our warning system: 'Whoever trusts in his own mind is a fool, but he who walks in wisdom will be delivered' (28:26). The clear guidance of Scripture often runs counter to our natural way of doing things. Maintaining sexual purity, controlling our speech, giving generously to others, etc., are not natural ways of living. Our desires and instincts pull us one way, but God-given wisdom helps us navigate safely the path of life.

What Do You Recommend?

Whether navigating the streets of a strange city or searching the woods for wildlife, the feeling of being lost is an experience common to life. Once, when Miriam was a freshman at Clemson, she and her friend, Beth Pollock, were late driving home for the weekend. I began to worry about them. Calling Miriam's cellphone, I asked, 'Where are you?' 'We're on Interstate 85', was her reply. 'What mile marker are you near?' 'We just passed mile marker 10.' Looking at a map, I said, 'Wait a minute. You're in Georgia!' Without a map or anyone with them who knew the way, they had gone south on I-85 instead of north. If they only had a compass, they might not been so confused.

[1] John MacArthur, *The Vanishing Conscience* (Dallas, TX: Word Publishing, 1994).

Proverbs encourages us to seek advice from others when making decisions. Consulting those with wisdom is a primary means of guidance:

• 'Where there is no guidance, a people falls, but in an abundance of counsellors there is safety' (11:14).

• 'The way of a fool is right in his own eyes, but a wise man listens to advice' (12:15).

• 'By insolence comes nothing but strife, but with those who take advice is wisdom' (13:10).

• 'Without counsel plans fail, but with many advisers they succeed' (15:22).

• 'Listen to advice and accept instruction, that you may gain wisdom in the future' (19:20).

• 'Plans are established by counsel; by wise guidance wage war' (20:18).

• 'for by wise guidance you can wage your war, and in abundance of counsellors there is victory' (24:6).

We should learn to seek advice for any major decision or undertaking. Notice how often we are admonished to seek many counsellors.

Not So Fast!

Often our worst mistakes result from our own presumption. We think we know exactly what needs to be done, or we feel we have no time to consult others or to seek the Lord's guidance, so we dash ahead. Glen Knecht said, 'The hardest lesson to learn is the one we thought we already knew.'

• 'There is a way that seems right to a man, but its end is the way to death' (14:12).

• 'The heart of man plans his way, but the LORD establishes his steps' (16:9).

• 'Desire without knowledge is not good, and whoever makes haste with his feet misses his way' (19:2).

Waiting on the Lord to open doors or to make clear the path we must take can be difficult, but the believer must learn patience. The example of Saul's impatience while waiting for God to guide him is a clear warning to every believer. Having gone to Gilgal and waited seven days as instructed by the prophet Samuel, Saul felt he could wait no longer. His enemies, the Philistines, were gathering for battle; his own troops, out of fear, were deserting him by the hour; and Samuel was nowhere to be seen! So taking the bull by the horns, literally, Saul usurped the role of priest and offered up sacrifices to God (which was contrary to God's law), in the vain hope that the Lord would show him what to do. Just then Samuel arrived on the scene and said, 'You have done foolishly. You have not kept the command of the LORD your God, with which he commanded you. For then the LORD would have established your kingdom over Israel forever. But now your kingdom shall not continue' (*1 Sam.* 13:13-14).

The short-cuts we take, the hasty conclusions we reach, often result in wasted effort or, worse still, unintended consequences. Though we all make mistakes, the rule of scale should govern our decision-making. Small decisions, such as where to eat supper, require little reflection; but big decisions, such as whom to marry, which school to attend, which job to take, require prayerful reflection. Study the word of God for clear, guiding principles. Seek counsel from an abundance of friends, family and other advisors. Spread the matter before the Lord (*2 Kings* 19:14). Pray over it diligently, and wait for a sense of peace and direction from the Lord. 'Behold, I pour out my spirit on you; I will make my words known to you' (*Prov.* 1:23). 'For the LORD gives wisdom; from his mouth come knowledge and understanding; he stores up sound wisdom for the upright; he is a shield to those who walk in integrity, guarding the paths of justice and watching over the way of his saints' (2:6-8). 'The LORD will be your confidence and will keep your foot from being caught' (3:26).

Summary

Reading the Bible and seeking the mind of Christ should be part of our daily routine. We never know when significant events or major decisions will be thrust upon us. Jesus is 'the way, and the truth, and the life' (*John* 14:6), so let us walk closely with him. The best way to receive guidance is to know the mind of the guide. 'Therefore do not be foolish, but understand what the will of the Lord is' (*Eph.* 5:17).

Key Principle: The Lord guides us by the principles revealed in his Word, by the provision or withholding of resources, by the counsel of others, and by the sanctified desires of our hearts.

9

PRIDE

Of all the deadly sins, Proverbs singles out pride as perhaps the most destructive. What is pride? How does it manifest itself? What if I really am the smartest? (Reality check!) What is the antidote for pride? Proverbs gives us the following answers and more.

High and Lifted Up

The basic Hebrew word for pride conveys the idea of 'lifted up'. Pride is nothing more than an inflated sense of self-worth and self-importance.

• 'Be not wise in your own eyes' (3:7). The truly wise person realizes how much he does not understand.

• 'Haughty eyes and a proud heart, the lamp of the wicked, are sin' (21:4). The opposite of a humble and gentle spirit is the person who radiates arrogance—a supercilious snarl on the lips, eyebrows raised in arrogance, looking down the nose at lesser mortals.

Proverbs calls it what it is—a sin. The Lord Jesus once told a parable to expose 'some who trusted in themselves that they were righteous, and treated others with contempt' (*Luke* 18:9). A religious leader and a tax-collector (the tax-collectors were renowned for cheating others) went to the temple to pray.

> The Pharisee, standing by himself, prayed thus: God, I thank you that I am not like other men, extortioners, unjust, adulterers, or even like this tax collector. I fast twice a week; I give tithes of all that I get.' But the tax collector, standing far off, would not even lift up his eyes to heaven, but beat his breast, saying, 'God, be merciful to me, a sinner!' I tell you, this man went down to his house justified, rather than the other. For everyone who exalts himself will be humbled, but the one who humbles himself will be exalted (*Luke* 18:11-14).

• '"Scoffer" is the name of the arrogant, haughty man who acts with arrogant pride' (*Prov.* 21:24). The truly arrogant not only think they are better than everybody else, but they treat others accordingly. When Cathy was young, her family kept a few goats on their farm. The dominant billy was a mean, old goat named LBJ (political pun intended), who viciously head-butted anyone who came near. The proud, haughty scoffer engages in the same sort of bullying. Like LBJ, they have a certain air about them.

Pride in Action

The proud person shows it in the way he speaks and acts around others.

• 'The poor use entreaties, but the rich answer roughly' (18:23). Proverbs compliments the person who lives in humble circumstances and treats others gently, but condemns the person of means who treats others condescendingly and is verbally abusive.

Riches can so easily breed an air of superiority in those who possess them.

• 'Do not put yourself forward in the king's presence or stand in the place of the great, for it is better to be told, "Come up here", than to be put lower in the presence of a noble' (25:6-7). This is the picture of a social climber, who takes the seat of honour at a public gathering, and must be asked to move further to the back when the honoured guests arrive.

• 'Like clouds and wind without rain is a man who boasts of a gift he does not give' (25:14). Any smart business person knows it is better to under-promise and over-perform than to boast falsely about what will be accomplished. You cannot build a reputation on what you are going to do.

• 'It is not good to eat much honey, nor is it glorious to seek one's own glory' (25:27). When a proud person starts boasting about his own accomplishments, or starts fishing for compliments from others, it is nauseating!

• 'Do you see a man who is wise in his own eyes? There is more hope for a fool than for him' (26:12). Given the choice between a pompous person or a fool as a marriage or business partner, take the fool.

• 'The sluggard is wiser in his own eyes than seven men who can answer sensibly' (26:16). The proud person can be so blinded by visions of his own glory that he cannot appreciate reality.

• 'Let another praise you, and not your own mouth; a stranger, and not your own lips' (27:2). Basically, every form of self-praise stinks.

• 'A rich man is wise in his own eyes, but a poor man who has understanding will find him out' (28:11). The successful person who mistakenly thinks his intellect, education, and life circumstances are self-generated, rather than gifts from God, does not truly understand. The poor person who has understanding sees right through him—and is far better off!

• 'If you have been foolish, exalting yourself . . . put your hand on your mouth' (30:32).

The person who seems better than everyone else, who seems to think he is the master of his own destiny, has established an idol for himself—*himself!* And he who has himself for a god has a very small god!

Here Comes the Judge!

Sports commentators often talk about a 'level playing field'. What they are referring to is parity, or an even match, between the competitors. In the game of life, there is one who will bring down the high and mighty, and exalt the lowly. God is the ultimate leveller.

• 'There are six things that the Lord hates, seven that are an abomination to him . . . haughty eyes' (6:16-17). The Lord's indignation is stirred in a special way by the arrogant, and they will get their come-uppance.

• 'The LORD tears down the house of the proud but maintains the widow's boundaries' (15:25). It is amazing to contemplate, but the Lord actively works against—and one day will utterly destroy—the proud, but he exercises his sovereign dominion to protect and deliver the powerless.

• 'Everyone who is arrogant in heart is an abomination to the LORD; be assured, he will not go unpunished' (16:5). Hubris is anathema to the Lord.

• 'Pride goes before destruction, and a haughty spirit before a fall' (16:18). This is one of the best-known Proverbs, and speaks eloquently of the disaster looming for the arrogant. The man with his nose in the air will eventually trip over his own shoe laces.

The Grace of Humility

The realization that there is no such thing as a self-made man is very liberating. Paul Boler[1] tells the story of Pennsylvania Congressman Thaddeus Stevens, who despised President Andrew Johnson. When a friend asserted that Johnson was a self-made man, Stevens responded, 'I never thought about it that way, but it does relieve God Almighty of a heavy responsibility!'

The logic of genuine humility is very simple. I did not create myself. I did not choose my race, hair colour, height, sex, or IQ. What is more, I cannot change the fundamental characteristics I was given. How, then, can I ever congratulate myself for how smart (or handsome, or rich, or . . .) I am? To do so is preposterous! God alone made me and sustains me.

Proverbs teaches clearly that humility—an honest estimation of self—is a characteristic the Lord loves. And he gives great blessings to the humble.

• 'When pride comes, then comes disgrace, but with the humble is wisdom' (11:2). The proud receive dishonour as a consequence of already knowing it all, but the Lord grants wisdom to the humble because they are teachable.

[1] Paul Boler, *Congressional Anecdotes* (Oxford: Oxford University Press, 1991), p. 280.

• 'The fear of the Lord is instruction in wisdom, and humility comes before honour' (15:33). Fearing the Lord leads to wisdom, and humility leads to honour. Wisdom and honour are the fruit of humility.

• 'Before destruction a man's heart is haughty, but humility comes before honour' (18:12). The long-term consequences are ironic: the proud man wants to be honoured, yet will be destroyed. The humble man knows he is not worthy of honour, yet he will be exalted.

• 'The reward for humility and fear of the Lord is riches and honour and life' (22:4). What more can one want?

• 'A greedy [or 'arrogant'] man stirs up strife, but the one who trusts in the Lord will be enriched' (28:25). The proud, trusting in their own way, get ruffled when all does not go according to their plan. The humble allow God to be God, and will prosper under his loving care.

• 'Whoever trusts in his own mind is a fool, but he who walks in wisdom will be delivered' (28:26). The one who does not seek the guidance and favour of the Lord, but rather does what is right in his own eyes, will come to ruin.

• 'One's pride will bring him low, but he who is lowly in spirit will obtain honour' (29:23). Pride is a dead-end street.

Summary

Proverbs makes a compelling case for every person to humbly submit their life to the Lord. Pride is a symptom of spiritual blindness, which in the end cripples and destroys the rich, the strong, the beautiful, and the intelligent, who are convinced they have these blessings by their own strength. Little gods they are, and little devils they will become.

Key Principle: Self-praise, whether spoken or unspoken, stinks.

10

HEALTH

Proverbs is by no means a practical manual on physical fitness. It does, however, recognize a connection between body and soul which is very important to understand. What is good for the soul tends to be good for the body, and vice versa.

Speak to Me

As we discussed in Chapter 4, Proverbs teaches that the power of life and death lies in the tongue (*Prov.* 18:21). The words we speak can either build up or destroy others. What is interesting, however, is how literally true this is. It is not just the emotions but the health of others we can build up or destroy:

• 'Anxiety in a man's heart weighs him down, but a good word makes him glad' (12:25). Good news and encouraging words have an uplifting effect on the hearer. This goodness works its way into the hearer's body and spirit.

• 'A tranquil heart gives life to the flesh, but envy makes the bones rot' (14:30). The writer of Proverbs knew long before electocardiographs and blood pressure cuffs were invented that stress is hard on the body.

• 'A glad heart makes a cheerful face, but by sorrow of heart the spirit is crushed' (15:13).

• 'The light of the eyes rejoices the heart, and good news refreshes the bones' (15:30).

• 'Gracious words are like a honeycomb, sweetness to the soul and health to the body' (16:24).

• 'A joyful heart is good medicine, but a crushed spirit dries up the bones' (17:22).

Notice how often joy appears in these verses. There can be no doubt that the life of faith, founded upon the good news of the gospel of Jesus Christ, and fuelled by the power of the Holy Spirit, is good for one's health. Introducing 'love, joy, peace, patience, kindness, goodness, faithfulness, gentleness, and self-control' into one's daily life is a recipe for health that only the Great Physician could have prescribed (*Gal.* 5:22-23).

Length of Days

The connection between righteous living (fearing the Lord and walking in his ways) and enjoying good health and length of days cannot be overlooked:

• 'My son, do not forget my teaching, but let your heart keep my commandments, for length of days and years of life and peace they will add to you' (3:1-2).

• 'Be not wise in your own eyes; fear the LORD, and turn away from evil. It will be healing to your flesh and refreshment to your bones' (3:7-8).

• 'Hear, my son, and accept my words, that the years of your life may be many' (4:10).

• 'My son, be attentive to my words; incline your ear to my sayings. Let them not escape from your sight; keep them within your heart. For they are life to those who find them, and healing to all their flesh' (4:20-,22).

• 'Grey hair is a crown of glory; it is gained in a righteous life' (16:31).

How does righteous living add to our span of life? In part it is practical: the person who does not drink alcohol excessively, eat gluttonously, drive recklessly, sleep with multiple sexual partners, or lead a violent life is far more likely to survive 'threescore years and ten'. When my mother-in-law, Ann Edwards (a registered nurse), sees a morbidly obese person, she routinely says, 'I don't think he'll make old bones.'

But to a certain degree also the connection between righteousness and longevity is spiritual. A clear conscience is healing to the body and soul. A guilty conscience destroys both. The stress and anxiety of holding onto sin, against the dictates of conscience and reason, is sure to destroy a person.

King David, father of Solomon, one of the principal writers of the book of Proverbs, knew first hand this connection between body and soul. After he had committed adultery with Bathsheba and had murdered her husband, Uriah the Hittite, David felt the hot hand of the Lord pressing upon his life and conscience. The shame and horror of his sin began to eat him alive. 'For I know my transgressions, and my sin is ever before me . . . Let me hear joy and gladness; let the bones that you have broken rejoice. Hide your face from my sins, and blot out all my iniquities' (*Psa.* 51:3, 8-9). Responding in faith to the word and promise of God by making an open confession of his sin put David on the road to restoration and recovery (*2 Sam.* 12:13-25). His 'broken bones' began to heal following his repentance.

Does the promise of Proverbs 3:1-2 mean that the Lord guarantees a certain number of years to every believer? Of course not. What it does mean is that the years granted will be sufficient for the believer to experience grace and to fulfil his or her particular calling to walk with the Lord in faithfulness. Moses, who lived a long and productive life, knew this well. He wrote, 'So teach us to number our days that we may get a heart of wisdom' (*Psa.* 90:12).

Bone of My Bones

The most intimate of human relationships, husband and wife, clearly has an impact on the health of the spouses. A strong marriage is beneficial for both body and soul, while a contentious marriage can be a ticket to an early grave.

- 'An excellent wife is the crown of her husband, but she who brings shame is like rottenness in his bones' (12:4).

- 'It is better to live in a desert land than with a quarrelsome and fretful woman' (21:19).

• 'It is better to live in a corner of the housetop than in a house shared with a quarrelsome wife' (25:24).

• 'An excellent wife who can find? She is far more precious than jewels. The heart of her husband trusts in her, and he will have no lack of gain. She does him good, and not harm, all the days of her life' (31:10-12).

• 'Her children rise up and call her blessed; her husband also, and he praises her: "Many women have done excellently, but you surpass them all"' (31:28-29).

Notice that the pattern is circular, or self-feeding. Words of praise make the heart glad and pleasant words are sweet to the soul. On the other hand, contentiousness and envy within a household break the spirit and are rottenness to the bones. How I speak to and treat my spouse over the years will determine, to a large degree, my own physical and spiritual wellbeing! 'In the same way husbands should love their wives as their own bodies. He who loves his wife loves himself. For no one ever hated his own flesh, but nourishes and cherishes it, just as Christ does the church' (*Eph.* 5:28-29).

Is it any wonder that after thirty or forty years of living together, husbands and wives usually show the effects of domestic life in their physical demeanour? Domestic peace produces a quiet joy and radiance. Domestic strife produces emotional and physical strain.

Summary

The connection between body and soul is significant. Spiritual health promotes physical health in many ways. Dr Abraham

Kuyper learned the art of promoting both simultaneously. He followed the strict habit of walking two hours per day, usually in the early evening, to keep himself physically fit, and to have time to think, pray and plan.[1] His eighty-three years of prodigious personal and professional accomplishments stand as a monument to the virtues of godly and healthy living.

Key Principle: Godly living is good for the body and soul.

---

[1] Frank Vanden Berg, *Abraham Kuyper*, (Grand Rapids, MI: Eerdmans, 1960).

11

KINDNESS AND MERCY

When the prophet Micah asked the all-important question, What does God require of man?, the answer given to him was straightforward: 'He has told you, O man, what is good; and what does the LORD require of you but to do justice, and to love kindness, and to walk humbly with your God?' (*Mic.* 6:8). What does the Lord mean when he says we are to 'love kindness'?

The Hebrew word rendered kindness here can also be translated as lovingkindness, mercy or compassion. The basic meaning of kindness is to be favourably disposed towards others. The greatest example of kindness is the covenant love the Lord has for his people, which manifests itself in his settled determination to do only and always what is in their best interest. It is an active, not passive, type of kindness. The Lord's unfailing, jealous love for his people is a fundamental fact of life, and both his children and his enemies need to understand the far-reaching implications of this truth. 'The LORD's curse is on the house of the wicked, but he blesses the dwelling of the righteous' (*Prov.* 3:33). 'A good man obtains favour from the LORD, but a man of evil devices he condemns' (12:2).

How do the 'righteous' and the 'good' treat others? With the same kindness and compassion they have received from the Lord.

The Twin Towers

Proverbs establishes a remarkable link between kindness and faithfulness.

• 'Let not steadfast love [kindness] and faithfulness forsake you; bind them around your neck; write them on the tablet of your heart' (3:3). The word rendered here as 'faithfulness' has a root meaning of stability (to build up or support). The fundamental way we treat others (kindness) and the consistency with which we do so (faithfulness) are to be the twin towers of our human relations. What kind of monument am I building with my life, measured by the way I treat people and the consistency of such kindness?

• 'Do they not go astray who devise evil? Those who devise good meet steadfast love and faithfulness' (14:22). Making it our aim to show kindness and faithfulness to others keeps us on track, and we receive similar treatment in return.

• 'By steadfast love and faithfulness iniquity is atoned for, and by the fear of the LORD one turns away from evil' (16:6). This does not mean that I can be good enough (kindness) and faithful enough to atone for my own sin. It means God in his own compassion and faithfulness spared me by the atoning work of his Son. But having been redeemed, I am to live accordingly. My own kindness and faithfulness are the consequences of this relationship, not the cause of it. Forgiveness is the origin of kindness.

The Atmosphere of Home

Dr Sinclair Ferguson, senior pastor of First Presbyterian Church of Columbia, South Carolina, likes to say, 'The children breathe in what the parents breathe out.' In other words, the atmosphere of the home—what we value, how we treat each other, what priority we place on walking with the Lord—is impressed on the hearts and minds of our children. Though we often view kindness and gentleness as feminine qualities, both father and mother play a key role in modelling kindness:

• 'What is desired in a man is steadfast love [kindness]' (19:22). Not his strength. Not his wealth. Not his chiselled physique and handsome features. Character is what counts. The reality is that true strength is displayed in gentleness, true wealth is displayed in generosity, and true attractiveness is displayed in favouring others over self. Many people ridiculed President George H. W. Bush when he said America should aspire to be 'a kinder, gentler nation'. But was he not correct?

• 'She opens her mouth with wisdom, and the teaching of kindness is on her tongue' (31:26). It is true that actions speak louder than words, but our words reflect what is in our heart. When the noble wife opens her mouth, the kindness in her heart becomes evident.

• 'Her children rise up and call her blessed; her husband also, and he praises her: "Many women have done excellently, but you surpass them all"' (31:28-29). Kindness expressed in words echoes around the house and builds on itself. The habit of speaking blessings to one another must begin with the father. How else would the children have learned to praise their mother?

Do unto Others

The Lord's kindness in dealing with us is intended to be the pattern for our treatment of others. Kindness is an inner disposition, an attitude toward others, which manifests itself in the words we speak and the actions we take. It is, broadly speaking, a desire for the wellbeing of others. Billy Graham once defined it as 'mildness in dealing with one another'.

Proverbs teaches us to be kind toward two particular groups of people: the poor and our enemies. Compassion toward one group is relatively easy to show, but being kind to the other requires, well, a lot of grace.

• 'Whoever oppresses a poor man insults his Maker, but he who is generous to the needy honours him' (14:31). If someone helps my child, they are honouring me in a very real sense. Likewise, if we help those in need, we are honouring their Creator.

• 'Whoever despises his neighbour is a sinner, but blessed is he who is generous to the poor' (14:21). How we treat the tired, the poor, the hungry, and the downtrodden speaks volumes about the kind of person we are. These folks can do us no good, in a sense, yet we are to show them kindness. One of my father-in-law's friends once told him, 'Don't waste your time with so-and-so, he's not rich enough to do you any good.' What arrogance!

• 'Do not rejoice when your enemy falls, and let not your heart be glad when he stumbles' (24:17). Not only my actions, but my attitudes, are important. True compassion knows no bounds, even for those who seek to harm me.

• 'If your enemy is hungry, give him bread to eat, and if he is thirsty, give him water to drink, for you will heap burning coals on his head, and the LORD will reward you' (25:21-22). The pangs of conscience (burning coals) may awaken him to his own need for forgiveness. But even if not, we are to be like our Father—loving our enemies and doing good things for them. This is the ultimate expression of the Golden Rule.

Summary

Proverbs teaches clearly the general principle of sowing and reaping; we reap what we sow. 'A man who is kind benefits himself, but a cruel man hurts himself' (11:17). But self-motivation alone is not enough. Without question we need the Lord's help to genuinely be kind and merciful to others. And God gives us the grace we need, for 'the fruit of the Spirit is . . . kindness . . . If we live by the Spirit, let us also walk by the Spirit' (*Gal.* 5:22, 25).

Key Principle: Kindness is a genuine desire for the wellbeing of others, expressed in our words and actions.

12

JUSTICE AND EQUITY

We are all familiar with the powerful image of Lady Justice, blindfolded, holding the scales of justice. The essence of justice is its blindness—no favouritism or prejudice. The Lord is a just God, and he demands justice and equity in the course of human affairs.

Justice is so essential that Proverbs begins with this explanation of why Solomon recorded his sayings: he wanted his readers 'to receive instruction in wise dealing, in righteousness, justice, and equity' (*Prov.* 1:3). In fact, God places such a premium on justice that he reminds us, that to 'do righteousness and justice is more acceptable to the LORD than sacrifice' (21:3). The Lord is far more interested in our obedience than in our religious observances. Without true obedience our religious exercises are meaningless and hypocritical ceremonies, mere form without substance.

What are the areas of life in which justice is demanded? Proverbs highlights three: commerce, law, and social responsibility.

Fair Dealings in Commerce

The marketplace is a common scene in all nations and cultures. Merchants display their wares, shoppers browse for the best bargain, and perhaps a little negotiation takes place before the deal is struck. Such transactions are completed over and over again around the world. The universal temptation for the seller is to enhance his profit by deception. A lighter weight on the scale, a smaller container for the measure, a different set of books for the tax man, and the bottom line grows. The rationalization is easy: everyone does it; the buyer will not know the difference; competition is so great I cannot survive unless I play the game aggressively. Yet someone is watching:

• 'Treasures gained by wickedness do not profit' (10:2).

• 'A false balance is an abomination to the LORD, but a just weight is his delight' (11:1).

• 'A just balance and scales are the LORD's; all the weights in the bag are his work' (16:11).

• 'Unequal weights and unequal measures are both alike an abomination to the LORD' (20:10).

• 'Unequal weights are an abomination to the LORD, and false scales are not good' (20:23).

The application of these warnings is almost endless. The child of God is to charge fair rates, deliver the goods or services promised, keep honest and complete records, and file accurate tax returns, to the best of his or her ability. Intentionally cutting corners will not profit in the end; obedience is the greatest long-term investment.

Law and Order

Human government is instituted by God for the welfare of mankind. 'Let every person be subject to the governing authorities. For there is no authority except from God, and those that exist have been instituted by God' (*Rom.* 13:1). In other words, government is God's agent to encourage good and to punish evil.

The essence of government's role is to promote justice, through the establishment and enforcement of laws. Both the design and the implementation of the laws must be fair and equitable, according to Proverbs.

• 'He who justifies the wicked and he who condemns the righteous are both alike an abomination to the LORD' (*Prov.* 17:15). The evil judge who favours the wicked and discriminates against the righteous strikes a very deep nerve with the Lord. Such things are an abomination—vile and intolerable—in his eyes.

• 'The wicked accepts a bribe in secret to pervert the ways of justice' (17:23). A bribe is a payment under the table to obtain favourable treatment or to induce action. In many cultures government and business routinely operate this way. The closest I ever came to bribing someone was in 1993 when Pastor Glen Knecht and I were travelling in Ukraine. Attempting to check into a hotel one night, we were told by the clerk he had no rooms available. Seeing a Russian Bible in my briefcase, however, the clerk told our translator that if we gave him the Bible he might be able to find a room. I didn't understand all that was said, but Glen and I checked into a room shortly thereafter, one Bible poorer! Ten rubles and one *biblio* seemed like a fair price to us.

• 'It is not good to be partial to the wicked or to deprive the righteous of justice' (18:5). Woe to the one who perverts justice—favouring the wicked and condemning the righteous.

• 'The one who states his case first seems right, until the other comes and examines him' (18:17). The wise judge listens to both sides of the story before jumping to conclusions. And after practising law for over twenty years, I've certainly learned there are two sides to every story!

• 'A worthless witness mocks at justice' (19:28). A false witness so taints the administration of justice that perjury is a punishable offence in its own right.

• 'A king who sits on the throne of justice disperses all evil with his eyes' (20:8). A king or judge with a reputation for justice is a strong deterrent to evil. The threat of punishment is sufficient to restrain a great deal of misconduct.

• 'When justice is done, it is a joy to the righteous but terror to evildoers' (21:15). The Apostle Paul understood this principle when he wrote, 'For rulers are not a terror to good conduct, but to bad. Would you have no fear of the one who is in authority? Then do what is good, and you will receive his approval . . . But if you do wrong, be afraid, for he does not bear the sword in vain' (*Rom.* 13:3-4).

• 'Partiality in judging is not good. Whoever says to the wicked, "You are in the right", will be cursed by peoples, abhorred by nations, but those who rebuke the wicked will have delight, and a good blessing will come upon them' (*Prov.* 24:23-25). The essence of a corrupt and unjust judge is the one who calls good evil and evil good.

• 'By justice a king builds up the land, but he who exacts gifts tears it down' (29:4). The leader sets the tone for his followers, and his level of integrity trickles down to the masses. As the shepherd goes, so goes the flock.

• 'An unjust man is an abomination to the righteous, but one whose way is straight is an abomination to the wicked' (29:27). This verse highlights the conflict between the kingdom of light and the kingdom of darkness which rages in the world. The crooked and the straight, the unjust and the just, are at war with one another. Do the right thing, and do not be surprised when the very good you have done is a source of criticism or comes under attack. The Lord will justify in the end.

Social Justice

Proverbs calls on every believer to defend the poor and those without power. The notion of social justice is deeply rooted in the Mosaic law, requiring the interests of the orphan, the widow, and the poor to be jealously guarded.

• 'The fallow ground of the poor would yield much food, but it is swept away through injustice' (13:23). The potential to meet the needs of the poor can be destroyed by injustice. The refusal to provide resources or opportunities to the poor when it is within our ability to do so is unjust. Not necessarily the provision of a handout, but the knowledge and opportunity to labour, is in view.

• 'Do not rob the poor, because he is poor, or crush the afflicted at the gate, for the LORD will plead their cause and rob of life those who rob them' (22:22-23). Exploiting the poor and the afflicted because they are easy prey is a huge and costly mistake.

• 'Do not move an ancient landmark or enter the fields of the fatherless, for their Redeemer is strong; he will plead their cause against you' (23:10). Stealing property or crops from an orphan because he seems defenceless is a gross miscalculation. The one with whom we must contend is too strong for us.

• 'A poor man who oppresses the poor is a beating rain that leaves no food' (28:3). Not only the wealthy but the poor must treat others fairly. Poverty is no excuse for injustice.

• 'A righteous man knows the rights of the poor; a wicked man does not understand such knowledge' (29:7). Those who pursue godliness are concerned for the rights of the poor, and take action accordingly. The wicked do not even understand such concern for others.

• 'The poor man and the oppressor meet together; the LORD gives light to the eyes of both' (29:13). Both the poor man and his arrogant oppressor have a Maker and Judge.

• 'Open your mouth for the mute, for the rights of all who are destitute. Open your mouth, judge righteously, defend the rights of the poor and needy' (31:8-9). When Cathy and I got involved in the fight to outlaw video poker in South Carolina in 1998, our motivation was to speak up for the rights of the poor and the afflicted whose families and financial worlds were being torn apart by addiction to gambling. The accusation of being self-appointed 'morality police' was thrown at us, but it was the right thing to do. The same reasoning applies to anti-abortion efforts to protect the lives of the unborn. The unborn have no voice; who will cry out for them?

• 'She opens her hand to the poor and reaches out her hands to the needy' (31:20). The virtuous woman is mindful of the less fortunate, and reaches out to meet their needs.

Summary

On a personal level, justice is not only a duty but brings great blessing. 'For the LORD gives wisdom; from his mouth come knowledge and understanding; he stores up sound wisdom for the upright; he is a shield to those who walk in integrity, guarding the paths of justice and watching over the way of his saints' (2:6-8). The child of God is to devote himself to searching God's word, acquiring God's wisdom, by which he can 'understand righteousness and justice and equity, every good path' (2:9).

But on a societal level, justice is also vital. We are to pray for our leaders—lawmakers, judges, law-enforcement officials—that the Lord would raise up godly men and women and put them in positions of authority, and would give wisdom and grace to those in office. 'If a king faithfully judges the poor, his throne will be established forever' (29:14).

In the end, we are to pursue justice because God is just. Knowing and emulating his character is what we are called to do. 'Evil men do not understand justice, but those who seek the LORD understand it completely' (28:5).

Key Principle: Justice demands that we speak for the poor, the defenceless and the oppressed.

13

AUTHORITY AND LEADERSHIP

Americans have grown noticeably hostile toward authority figures in the last fifty years. Since the 1950s, when members
of the so-called 'greatest generation' were running the country and
raising their families, rejection of the establishment has taken on
epic proportions. Presidents, parents, and pastors were once re-
spected, even if disliked. No longer.

The rallying cry of the 1960s was 'Question Authority'. The
self-absorbed 'Me' generation of the '70s led to the self-indulgent
'Material' generation of the '80s and '90s. The weakening of our
social institutions has been profound. In the common parlance,
many young people today have serious 'respect issues' with parents,
teachers, pastors, bosses and authority figures in general. How do
we reverse the decline?

All authority has been established by the Lord to benefit and
safeguard mankind. There are four key areas of life with God-ordained authority structures: the family, government, employment,
and the church. The specific leadership responsibilities within the
family are addressed in Chapters 14 and 15, but the general leadership principles found in the book of Proverbs apply broadly to all

of these. The person who questions God-ordained authority and refuses to live within its boundaries is in grave danger.

The Importance of Leadership

The effect a leader can have on those who follow is significant. So significant, in fact, that we can say, 'As the shepherd goes, so goes the flock.' For better or worse, the tone established by the leader eventually filters down to the followers. Though Proverbs usually speaks in terms of the 'king', the same principles apply to the parent, the elected official, the pastor, and the boss. What impact do these leaders have?

• 'A king who sits on the throne of judgment winnows all evil with his eyes' (20:8). The leader who rules firmly and justly will see the rats scamper from the room.

• 'A wise king winnows the wicked and drives the wheel over them' (20:26). The leader's job is to search out the malcontents and the malefactors, and deal with them appropriately.

• 'Steadfast love and faithfulness preserve the king, and by steadfast love his throne is upheld' (20:28). The positive side of a leader's mandate is to rule with covenant love for his people, and faithfulness; the result of which is the firm establishment of his position.

• 'When a land transgresses, it has many rulers, but with a man of understanding and knowledge, its stability will long continue' (28:2). Wicked and weak rulers tend to come and go frequently, bringing instability to the land. Righteous and strong leaders, on the other hand, provide moral stability. Derek Kidner notes: 'In just over two centuries, northern Israel, for its sins, had nine dynasties, each, after the first, inaugurated by an assassination. In three-and-a-half centuries, Judah, for David's sake, had only one.'[1]

• 'When the righteous triumph, there is great glory, but when the wicked rise, people hide themselves' (28:12). Wicked, self-serving rulers bring a cloud over the people, who then hide from his irrational wrath and greedy schemes. I once worked in an office with an angry, profane boss who regularly berated and bullied his staff. All the employees hid in their offices to avoid the storm of his fury—and secretly rejoiced when he got sick and died!

• 'Like a roaring lion or a charging bear is a wicked ruler over a poor people' (28:15). Ditto!

• 'When the wicked rise, people hide themselves, but when they perish, the righteous increase' (28:28). How many times this concept is repeated!

• 'When the righteous increase, the people rejoice, but when the wicked rule, the people groan' (29:2). The followers generally recognize and rejoice in righteous leaders.

• 'If a ruler listens to falsehood, all his officials will be wicked' (29:12). The leader sets the moral tone for the organization. If he tolerates (or encourages) bribes, lies and short-cuts, the rest of the people below him will follow suit.

Note that in all these Proverbs it is moral character, not intellect, charisma, or made-for-television good looks, that distinguishes a good leader. In his best-selling book, *Good to Great,* Jim Collins studied hundreds of publicly-traded companies to find out what

[1] Kidner, p. 168.

made a handful of them great performers. His conclusion:

> We were surprised, shocked really, to discover the type of leadership required for turning a good company into a great one. Compared to high-profile leaders with big personalities who make headlines and become celebrities, the good-to-great leaders seem to have come from Mars. Self-effacing, quiet, reserved, even shy—these leaders are a paradoxical blend of personal humility and professional will. They are more like Lincoln and Socrates than Patton or Caesar.[2]

Is it not amazing that even a purely secular study of success-ful businesses would so resoundingly verify the eternal truth of Scripture? Collins' conclusion that the greatest leaders 'are a study in duality: modest and willful, humble and fearless'[3] is exactly what Proverbs has been saying. The true measure of a successful leader is not the quality of the head, but the tone of the body. The leader who 'never let[s] his ego get in the way of his primary ambition for the larger cause', seeking first the wellbeing of the flock, will prosper. Which brings us to the next leadership principle from Proverbs.

Commander, Rule Yourself

Proverbs teaches that the first duty of a leader is to govern him-self. Leadership is not a license for self-gratification. The position of authority carries a duty to set aside self-interest and self-indul-gence, and to seek first the wellbeing of the organization and its members. Otherwise, a lack of respect and ultimately a rejection of his authority by the followers will result.

• 'An oracle is on the lips of a king; his mouth does not sin in judgment' (16:10). The leader must recognize the weight of re-

[2] Jim Collins, *Good to Great,* (NY: HarperCollins Publishers, 2001), pp. 12-13.
[3] Ibid., p. 22.

sponsibility on his shoulders, and not act carelessly or thoughtlessly. With power comes a burden.

• 'It is an abomination to kings to do evil, for the throne is established by righteousness' (16:12). The wicked ruler will quickly lose respect among his followers.

• 'The terror of a king is like the growling of a lion; whoever provokes him to anger forfeits his life' (20:2). The leader has a responsibility not to bare his claws at the slightest provocation, but, rather, must be patient and longsuffering.

• 'A ruler who lacks understanding is a cruel oppressor, but he who hates unjust gain will prolong his days' (28:16). The leader who rules by fear and intimidation is foolish—lacking an understanding of how God works. The leader who rules with integrity, on the other hand, will be blessed.

• 'By justice a king builds up the land, but he who exacts gifts tears it down' (29:4). The leader must restrain himself from unethical conduct, or else his flaws will destroy the entire fabric of the organization.

• 'If a king faithfully judges the poor, his throne will be established forever' (29:14). The poor can do the least to threaten or influence a king, therefore how well he treats them is a true measure of his integrity.

• 'Under three things the earth trembles; under four it cannot bear up: a slave when he becomes king . . .' (30:21). The leader, especially after a sudden rise to power, must maintain humility and self-control.

• 'Do not give your strength to women, your ways to those who destroy kings' (31:3). The ruler may have many pleasurable pastimes, privileges and distractions at his disposal, but he must stay focused on the mission. King David learned this the painful way with Bathsheba (*2 Sam.* 11).

• 'It is not for kings, O Lemuel, it is not for kings to drink wine, or for rulers to take strong drink, lest they drink and forget what has been decreed and pervert the rights of all the afflicted' (31:4-5). The leader must exercise great self-control in the consumption of alcohol (or any other judgment-altering substance), or else his carelessness may bring harm to many.

Our Lord and Saviour said that he had come to serve, not to be served. And so it should be with every effective leader. 'When one rules justly over men, ruling in the fear of God, he dawns on them like the morning light, like the sun shining forth on a cloudless morning, like rain that makes grass to sprout from the earth' (*2 Sam.* 23:3-4).

Listen Up!

Even the most experienced and capable leader needs guidance. Proverbs teaches that a wise leader surrounds himself with the right kind of advisors.

• 'The way of a fool is right in his own eyes, but a wise man listens to advice' (12:15). The leader who thinks he knows it all is certain to march right off a cliff. He must actively seek and follow wise counsel.

• 'Whoever walks with the wise becomes wise, but the companion of fools will suffer harm' (13:20). The character, values, and experience of our companions eventually wear off on us. Again the leader is warned to choose his companions carefully.

• 'Righteous lips are the delight of a king, and he loves him who speaks what is right' (16:13). Honest, direct advisors are essential. The leader who surrounds himself with 'yes' men merely listens to the echo of his own voice. The moral implications of a decision, not the political fallout, should be the primary concern of advisors and advisee alike.

• 'Take away the wicked from the presence of the king, and his throne will be established in righteousness' (25:5). Immoral, wicked individuals, though never beyond the hope of redemption, should never be seated next to the chairman. Leaders, like everyone else, become like the people in whose company they spend time. (See Chapter 3.)

• 'Like an archer who wounds everyone is one who hires a passing fool or drunkard' (26:10). The leader who carelessly hires the next warm body who comes through the door will regret it. Thoroughly check the background and references of prospective employees or advisors.

Follow the Leader

Proverbs teaches not only the leaders, but also the followers, a few principles about good citizenship. Whether as a member of a family or church, or a citizen or an employee, followers have certain responsibilities as well.

• 'A king's wrath is a messenger of death, and a wise man will appease it' (16:14). The follower is advised here to know his leader's hot buttons, so to speak, and avoid them. This does not mean to compromise values or avoid confrontation when appropriate, but to generally know the leader's agenda and be a good follower.

• 'In the light of a king's face there is life, and his favour is like the clouds that bring the spring rain' (16:15). A good follower is diligent to advance the organization's objectives, and appropriately receives the favour and blessings of the leader.

• 'A king's wrath is like the growling of a lion, but his favour is like dew on the grass' (19:12). The choice generally rests with the follower, whether to incur the wrath or the favour of the leader.

• 'The king's heart is a stream of water in the hand of the LORD; he turns it wherever he will' (21:1). Because all leaders need divine wisdom and guidance, the people everywhere are to pray for their leaders. If a wicked ruler takes office, fret not; for they, too, are in God's hands.

• 'My son, fear the LORD and the king' (24:21). This mandate for good citizenship was echoed in Peter's charge to honour the king as part of the pursuit of godliness (1 Pet. 2:17).

• 'Many seek the face of a ruler, but it is from the LORD that a man gets justice' (29:26). We must not look upon human leaders as our saviours. Ultimately, justice comes from the hand of the Lord.

Being a good follower is a skill, like being a good leader. Dr Jonathan King, a deacon at First Presbyterian Church, tells the story of being dissatisfied with the way his pastor at a prior church was handling a matter. Going to one of the elders for advice, Jonathan was told he just needed to be quiet and be a good follower. Jonathan saw the wisdom in the older man's advice, and did so. He says it was a very valuable lesson.

Summary

Godly leadership is instituted by God as a means of protecting and guiding his people. Recognizing and honouring all proper lines of authority brings abundant blessing to the follower.

Key Principle: God places authorities over us in all areas of life, to protect and guide us. Respect all authority in government, family, employment, and church.

14

Husband and Father

The proudest moment of my life was around 7:30 pm on Friday, June 26, 1981, when Cathy slipped that gold wedding band onto my finger. Though merely a symbol, it signified a greater reality—that I was now a husband, bound in covenant love to my dear wife. Other major life events would follow—the birth of our children, law school graduation, etc. Though each was extremely significant, all fall secondary to my life's primary calling to be a faithful husband to my wife.

Proverbs teaches basic principles about the role of a man as husband and father.

Leave and Cleave

The marriage relationship is the most significant and intimate relationship in one's life. Proverbs holds a high regard for the institution of marriage, and articulates the blessings of holy matrimony.

• 'Let your fountain be blessed, and rejoice in the wife of your youth, a lovely deer, a graceful doe. Let her breasts fill you at all times with delight; be intoxicated always in her love' (5:18-19). Speaking here of the joys and comforts of physical love, God encourages and blesses a healthy and robust sexual relationship between husband and wife. The words used in this passage are remarkable: 'blessed', 'rejoice', 'delight', and 'intoxicated'. Exclusivity ('yourself alone') and faithfulness ('not for strangers', cf. verse 17) breed exhilaration. (See Chapter 5.)

• 'He who finds a wife finds a good thing and obtains favour from the LORD' (18:22). Kidner notes that 'after wisdom itself, the best of God's blessings is a good wife.'[1] Subsequent Proverbs make clear that not every wife qualifies as a blessing. Some are a boon, others a bane.

• 'House and wealth are inherited from fathers, but a prudent wife is from the LORD' (19:14). In this life there are routine blessings—houses and wealth—and then there are extraordinary blessings—a prudent wife. Any father can give his children the former; only the heavenly Father can give his children the latter.

• 'Like a bird that strays from its nest is a man who strays from his home' (27:8). An iron-clad commitment to stick together through thick and thin is essential for a marriage to flourish. Though this Proverb does not specify whether the man is deserting wife or children or both, his primary failure must be to his vow of lifelong fidelity to his wife. The covenant of marriage is a commitment to mutually nurture and cherish 'til death do us part', and to walk away from it is as unnatural as a mother bird deserting her nest.

• 'An excellent wife who can find? She is far more precious than jewels. The heart of her husband trusts in her, and he will have no

---

[1] Kidner, p. 130.

lack of gain. She does him good, and not harm, all the days of her life' (31:10-12). An excellent wife is one who is righteous, diligent, and faithful, both to God and to her husband. Her husband trusts her, never doubts her integrity and faithfulness, and encourages her to be all she can be. As she prospers, so he prospers. She is his most precious treasure.

• 'Her children rise up and call her blessed; her husband also, and he praises her: "Many women have done excellently, but you surpass them all"' (31:28-29). The wife depicted in Proverbs 31 is worthy of her husband's praise. The Puritan commentator, Matthew Henry, cautions young men to seek first a woman of godly character and abiding virtue:

> He that designs to marry ought to seek diligently for such a one, to have this principally in [mind] in all his enquiries, and to take heed that he be not biased by beauty or gaiety, wealth or parentage, dressing well or dancing well; for all these things may be and yet the woman not be virtuous, and there is many a woman truly virtuous who yet is not [accompanied] by these advantages.[2]

Note also that the husband does not simply appreciate her virtues, admiring them in silence, but he speaks up and sings her praises.

It is unfortunate that marriage is increasingly deferred, disparaged and discarded in our society. The unwillingness to embrace lifelong commitment to one mate is a testament to the self-centredness of our age. The inability to commit at all, let alone early in adulthood, is a sign of misplaced priorities. The idea that one must complete his or her education, establish a career, see the world, and sample a host of relationships before 'settling down' is robbing many young men and women of one of life's greatest blessings. It is

---

[2] Matthew Henry, *Commentary on the Whole Bible*, (MacLean, VA: MacDonald Publishing Company, n.d.), Volume III, page 974.

not good to be alone, and it is time for men to respond to the call to pursue biblical marriage.

The goal of marriage is oneness, as described in Chapter 5, and the call of a husband is to 'sanctify' his wife by loving her unconditionally and drawing out the very best in her. (See Eph. 6: 25-29). To do so takes a steady commitment of effort over the long haul, and the sacrificing of other things that stand in the way. Yet doing so is the greatest blessing on earth. Choose faithfulness!

I Now Pronounce You Father

I almost failed Sociology 101 in college—I never understood a word my professor said! Now, thirty years later, some of the basic social concepts make a little more sense. Like fatherhood. Even a layman like me can see that there are various levels at which a man can be a father:

1. Biological

Just because you can sire babies does not mean you are a father. The man who has no relationship with his children is basically just a sperm donor.

2. Provider

This man goes to work and provides his family with the necessities of life: a roof over their heads and food on the table. This is a good start, but without doing more he still is not a true father.

3. Disciplinarian

Some fathers view themselves primarily as an authority figure, whose job is to beat the mischief out of the kids. The kind of father who rules the roost with an iron fist, squelching childish misbehaviour and snuffing out rebellion in his offspring, can succeed for a while. But eventually his children become bigger than he is, and develop the ability to tune him out.

4. Teacher

Now we are beginning to approach true fatherhood. The man who spends time with his kids and instills in them the core values and beliefs to be happy, productive citizens, so to speak, is worthy of the title 'Dad'. It takes both words and actions for the children to learn that dad really cares.

5. Mentor

The real goal is to be a mentor—someone who cherishes the relationship with his children, knows them well—their strengths and weaknesses—and helps them identify and pursue their life's calling. This man is like a beloved coach who is in equal parts instructor, motivator, and role model. I now pronounce you *father!*

Duties of a Father

Home is the greenhouse in which young ones are to be nurtured, trained, corrected and equipped for life, and fathers have the responsibility of being the master gardener. Proverbs gives fathers a comprehensive job description:

1. Lead your children to the Lord.

- 'The fear of the LORD is the beginning of knowledge; fools despise wisdom and instruction. Hear, my son, your father's instruction, and forsake not your mother's teaching' (1:7-8). A true father desires the best for his children, and this begins with a vital relationship with God. With such spiritual training, everything else in their life will fall in place. Without such spiritual training, nothing else in their life ultimately matters. My father-in-law recently recounted at a Thanksgiving gathering how his grandfather, Joseph Hooker Hieronymus, sat him down as a young boy of about five years of age and led him to Christ. Those conversations at Papa Hi's 'prayer tree' on the family farm in eastern Kentucky were a grandfather's greatest blessing to future generations.

• 'My son, if you receive my words and treasure up my commandments with you . . . then you will understand the fear of the LORD and find the knowledge of God' (2:1, 5). A loving father is diligent and intentional about teaching his children, giving them sayings and commandments—little proverbs—to live by. Recently I heard my 80-year-old father-in-law say, 'Dad always said . . .' Lessons taught by his father in the 1930s and '40s are as true and helpful today as when they were first spoken. I hope my children and grandchildren will do the same in another sixty or seventy years' time!

• 'My son do not forget my teaching, but let your heart keep my commandments . . . So you will find favour and good success in the sight of God and man' (3:1, 4). Generally speaking, obedience to God also brings favour with man. Certainly this is not true of those who are persecuted for their faith. Nevertheless, basic characteristics of honesty, diligence, loyalty, etc., will stand them in good stead in this world.

• 'My son . . . keep sound wisdom and discretion, and they will be life for your soul . . . For the LORD will be your confidence' (3:21, 22, 26). A father's heart desires that his children walk confidently and steadfastly with God. Seeing to the prosperity of their souls is far more important than anything else a father can do for his children.

• 'The fear of the LORD is the beginning of wisdom' (9:10). Reverence for the Lord is lesson No. 1. Wisdom will follow.

• 'That your trust may be in the LORD, I have made them known to you today, even to you' (22:19). A father never loses sight of the primary goal—that his children learn to trust in the Lord.

2. Be a gentle, consistent disciplinarian and teacher.

• 'For the LORD reproves him whom he loves, as a father the son in whom he delights' (3:12). The father who delights in his children will discipline them.

• 'When I was a son with my father, tender, the only one in the sight of my mother, he taught me and said to me, "Let your heart hold fast my words; keep my commandments, and live. Get wisdom"' (4:3-5). The spiritual conversations between father and child should begin early in life. Do not wait until the child is ready to leave the nest to begin teaching the most important thing. By then it is too late.

• 'My son, keep your father's commandment . . . For the commandment is a lamp and the teaching a light, and the reproofs of discipline are the way of life' (6:20, 23). Every child needs a lamp to light the way. A father can do nothing better than to show him the way of life.

• 'Hear, my son, and accept my words, that the years of your life may be many' (4:10). This general rule makes sense—clean living and good behaviour tend to add years to one's life. Not to mention peace and satisfaction.

• 'Whoever spares the rod hates his son, but he who loves him is diligent to discipline him' (13:24). The emphasis here is on the father's love and diligence. It is not anger but love that motivates a father to consistently monitor and correct his children's behaviour. Consistency of effort is critical, as is the measured level of discipline. Over-reaction or inconsistent enforcement of rules can frustrate and anger the child. The goal is to break the child's disobedience without breaking his spirit.

• 'Discipline your son, for there is hope; do not set your heart on putting him to death' (19:18). The father who 'loves' his child so much that he cannot bring himself to discipline the youngster, ironically brings about his child's death. David failed to discipline his fourth son, Adonijah. The young man was handsome and became proud, and wanted to usurp his father's throne, but the error of his ways brought about a violent death. 'His father [David] had never at any time displeased him by asking, "Why have you done thus and so?"' (1 Kings 1:6). Likewise, the priest Eli had two evil sons, Hophni and Phinehas, who also served as priests, but inwardly they were worthless hypocrites. The young men selfishly stole sacrifices from the worshippers who came to the temple, slept with the women who served at the temple, and generally despised the things of God. Eli saw their gluttony, lust and spiritual poverty, but never disciplined them. Finally God determined to put Eli and his sons to death, 'because his sons were blaspheming God, and he did not restrain them' (*1 Sam.* 3:13).

• 'Train up a child in the way he should go; even when he is old he will not depart from it' (22:6). This is one of the best-known and most often quoted Proverbs. It's truth is timeless—life's early lessons stick with us.

• 'Folly is bound up in the heart of a child, but the rod of discipline drives it far from him' (22:15). All children are born with sinful, self-centred natures. This is what theologians call original sin. A father's job is to teach his child the way of obedience.

• 'Do not withhold discipline from a child; if you strike him with a rod, he will not die. If you strike him with the rod, you will save his soul from Sheol' (23:13-14). The idea of corporal punishment is vehemently opposed by many self-styled 'experts' today, but their approach defies the timeless truth of Scripture and the wisdom that comes with experience. A child may wail when punished, but such correction is vital for his soul. Physical punishment must be administered in a measured fashion, but sometimes calling 'time out' or having an intellectual conversation about being obedient just is not enough.

• 'My son, if your heart is wise, my heart too will be glad. My inmost being will exult when your lips speak what is right' (23:15-16). The goal is to teach the children to think and act wisely on their own. A sense of 'mission accomplished' comes over a father who sees his child do or say the right thing without having to be prompted.

• 'The rod and reproof give wisdom, but a child left to himself brings shame to his mother . . . Discipline your son, and he will give you rest; he will give delight to your heart' (29:15, 17). Spoiled children are no pleasure for anyone to be around—especially if they are over forty!

3. Insist on respect.

There are several Proverbs which highlight the need for children to respect their parents. Obviously this is something the parents must teach their children—it does not just happen.

• 'A wise son makes a glad father, but a foolish man despises his mother' (15:20). I believe the father must set the tone of respect in a household—loving and respecting his wife and insisting that the children do the same. Amazingly, I've seen families in which the husband actively undercut the wife's authority—overruling her decisions or belittling her attitudes or actions—and then was surprised when the kids grew up to despise or neglect their mother. The father taught them to disrespect her by his own actions!

• 'He who does violence to his father and chases away his mother is a son who brings shame and reproach' (19:26). The unappreciative child who bullies his father or cuts off his mother is a shame and a disgrace.

• 'If one curses his father or his mother, his lamp will be put out in utter darkness' (20:20). A special level of punishment is reserved for the child who, far from benign neglect of his parents, actually curses them. Interestingly, what usually happens is that his own children will do the same to him in later life. The cycle of dysfunctional family relationships can be broken by grace. Teach your children to pronounce blessings, not curses, on their parents and siblings.

• 'Listen to your father who gave you life, and do not despise your mother when she is old' (23:22). Fathers should actively teach their children to hold a long-term view of family relationships—continuing to seek their father's counsel and to cherish and care for their mother in old age. This truth is bound up in the fifth commandment—'Honour your father and your mother, that your days may be long in the land that the LORD your God is giving you' (*Exod.* 20:12). The blessings of a multi-generational network of love and support cannot be overstated.

• 'There are those who curse their fathers and do not bless their mothers' (30:11). These are flip sides of the same coin—cursing and refusing to bless one's parents amount to the same thing.

• 'The eye that mocks a father and scorns to obey a mother will be picked out by the ravens of the valley and eaten by the vultures' (30:17). We have all seen a teenager roll the eyes when mom or dad says something they do not want to hear. Apparently such behaviour was common in ancient Israel as well. This vivid Proverb is timeless.

4. *Leave your children an inheritance—both spiritual and financial.*

A godly father blesses his children by bequeathing to them a dual legacy: a good name and an inheritance.

• 'A good man leaves an inheritance to his children's children, but the sinner's wealth is laid up for the righteous' (13:22). The lesson here is that the godly father has carefully saved his resources and wisely planned for the future, so he has resources available at life's end to leave to his family. The emphasis is not on the wealth itself in absolute measure, but on the godly act of providing a blessing for one's descendants. 'House and wealth are inherited from fathers' (19:14). The normal progression of life is for the older generation to pass along an inheritance to the next generation. Again, the emphasis is not on the security found in wealth but on the blessing that lies in the integrity of the family structure.

• 'An inheritance gained hastily in the beginning will not be blessed in the end' (20:21). A wise father teaches his children financial management along the way, rather than waiting until life's end and dropping an estate into their hands. Having spent my legal career as a specialist in wills, trusts and estates, I've observed that an inheritance is only a blessing if the descendants first have been trained to carefully manage their wealth and wisely use it.

• 'A good name is to be chosen rather than great riches' (22:1). Let there be no doubt that the best inheritance a father can leave his children is not a financial one. A good name is more desirable than great wealth, both for the father himself and for his posterity.

• 'He who loves wisdom makes his father glad, but a companion of prostitutes squanders his wealth' (29:3). A father's responsibility is to teach his children to value wisdom over wealth, and eternal prosperity over fleeting pleasure. I've seen many a prodigal son who wasted his inheritance on wine, women and song, breaking his parents' hearts in the process.

5. Be a godly example.

One of the best things a father can give his children and grandchildren is the tangible example of a life well spent.

• 'Grandchildren are the crown of the aged, and the glory of children is their fathers' (17:6). Godly fathers set in motion a chain of generational blessings. This Proverb lifts up the ideal of mutual love and admiration that runs back and forth between a grandfather and his offspring. A running joke in my wife's family is how much they all love to 'sit around and admire each other'. It is a beautiful thing to see three or four generations of family members regularly encouraging and enjoying each other.

• 'The righteous who walks in his integrity- blessed are his children after him!' (20:7). One of the greatest blessings a man can leave his children is his own integrity. The good name, community respect, and pattern of faithfulness left in his wake will bless his sons and daughters for generations to follow.

Summary

Being a husband and father are two of life's greatest callings. A wise man loves and cherishes his wife faithfully, and draws out the very best in her. As a father, he leads and teaches his children diligently, by God's grace.

Key Principle: A wise man is a faithful companion to his wife and a diligent mentor to his children.

15

WIFE AND MOTHER

Barefoot and pregnant. That's the image our culture has paint-
ed of the 'suppressed' role of women in the Bible. Proverbs
explodes that myth, and elevates the status of the woman who
becomes a wife and mother. Matrimony and maternity are high
callings, ordained by God, for the mutual wellbeing of men and
women. The biblical model of marriage is not merely about surviv-
ing, but thriving.

Our culture confuses a person's role with a person's worth. The
world says a president is more important than a vice-president,
when in reality every person is of intrinsic worth. A person's success or failure is measured by how well they do their job, not by
the job they are called to perform. Scripture teaches that God the
Father and God the Son were equal in status and worth, yet one of
them took a subservient role in order to perform a vital function.
'Have this mind among yourselves, which is yours in Christ Jesus,
who, though he was in the form of God, did not count equality
with God a thing to be grasped, but made himself nothing, taking
the form of a servant, being born in the likeness of men' (*Phil.* 2:
5-7).

There are elements of role distinction found in the biblical model of marriage. Embracing oneness in marriage, exercising one's gifts and abilities, and fulfilling one's calling are the choices that bless and satisfy.

An Excellent Wife

Proverbs 31 catalogues the virtues of an 'excellent wife' with the robust portrait of a godly, wise and diligent woman. What virtues mark her life?

1. She Fears the Lord.

A godly wife is a believer first and a wife second. Her relationship with God is her first priority, enabling all other relationships and pursuits to truly prosper. Though we tend to look for external characteristics like beauty and charm, Proverbs warns us to look first at the heart. 'Charm is deceitful, and beauty is vain, but a woman who fears the LORD is to be praised' (31:30). External beauty will fade with time, but the soul of the believer goes from strength to strength. True beauty, therefore, is an inner quality. 'Like a gold ring in a pig's snout is a beautiful woman without discretion' (11:22). When our oldest daughter, Miriam, was about three years old, Cathy and I tried to drill into her head the importance of being 'pretty on the inside'. One day we saw her push another child off the swing set in the yard. Snatching her up, Cathy reminded her that little girls need to act pretty on the inside. Miriam quickly retorted with a sly little smirk, 'But we were outside!' The wise woman cultivates a godly character first, and that inner beauty radiates outward for all to see.

X
2. *She Builds up Her Husband and Family.*

In her relationship with her husband, 'She does him good, and not harm, all the days of her life' (31:12). Every wife faces a multitude of small choices in her marriage. Will she build him up, or tear him down? Will she encourage him, help him and improve him, or let him get by on his own? Will she speak well of him to others, or belittle and undercut him? Because of her diligence and assistance, 'Her husband is known in the gates when he sits among the elders of the land' (31:23). Every marriage has its own chemistry, based on the personalities, gifts and goals of each spouse, but the strongest ones are marked by a supportive and encouraging wife. The wise woman chooses to faithfully build up her marriage, without letting selfishness or neglect destroy its foundation. 'The wisest of women builds her house, but folly with her own hands tears it down' (14:1).

X   Part of building up her marriage is a wife's commitment to faithfulness. The scourge of depravity and death is reserved for 'the forbidden woman, from the adulteress with her smooth words, who forsakes the companion of her youth and forgets the covenant of her God' (2:16-17). The brazen and rebellious woman who seduces naïve young men, leading them down the path of mutual destruction, is carried away by her own lust. 'Come, let us take our fill of love till morning; let us delight ourselves with love. For my husband is not at home; he has gone on a long journey . . . With much seductive speech she persuades him; with her smooth talk she compels him' (7:18-19, 21). The opposite of such a harlot is beautifully portrayed in Proverbs as a faithful and committed wife, satisfied with her husband's love. 'Let your fountain be blessed, and rejoice in the wife of your youth, a lovely deer, a graceful doe. Let her breasts fill you at all times with delight; be intoxicated always in her love' (5:18-19). This same passion is expressed by the bride in the Song of Solomon, when she says, 'let us go out early to the vineyards . . . There I will give you my love' (*Song of Sol.* 7:12).

The faithful wife who builds up her husband gains his unfailing trust and respect. As she moves about the marketplace, negotiating with merchants, or serves in the community, extending her hands to the poor, 'The heart of her husband trusts in her' (31:11). What is more, he lavishes her with praise, saying, 'Many women have done excellently, but you surpass them all' (31:29). In short, she is a blessing to her husband, and he recognizes and praises her for it.

In the end, it all boils down to choices. A wife must constantly choose between wisdom and folly. A virtuous wife is the greatest blessing, and a foolish wife the greatest curse, a man can ever receive. 'An excellent wife is the crown of her husband, but she who brings shame is like rottenness in his bones' (12:4).

3. She Spends Her Time Wisely.

The excellent wife of Proverbs 31 fills her days with constructive pursuits. In all these activities, her diligence and kindness are noteworthy.

Diligence

Though her ultimate priorities are her relationship with God, with her husband, and with her children, the wise woman diligently exercises her gifts and abilities. She provides for her household (verse 13), administers her staff (verse 15), negotiates with merchants and invests in property (verse 16), volunteers in the community (verse 20), and sells the fine goods she produces (verse 24). She rises early (verse 15) and stays up late (verse 18), looking after the needs of her family. 'She looks well to the ways of her household and does not eat the bread of idleness' (31:27). Her diligent efforts pay dividends many times over, and she earns high praise.

'Give her of the fruit of her hands, and let her works praise her in the gates' (31:31).

Kindness

An attractive quality in a wife is her kindness. 'She opens her hand to the poor and reaches out her hands to the needy' (31:20). Not only her actions, but her words, are dripping with genuine kindness toward others. 'She opens her mouth with wisdom, and the teaching of kindness is on her tongue' (31:26). Importantly, her kindness is not reserved for strangers, but begins within her own home. The home environment is the mutual responsibility of both spouses, but Proverbs minces no words about the unpleasantness of a contentious wife. 'Better is a dry morsel with quiet than a house full of feasting with strife' (17:1). 'It is better to live in a desert land than with a quarrelsome and fretful woman' (21:19). 'A continual dripping on a rainy day and a quarrelsome wife are alike; to restrain her is to restrain the wind or to grasp oil in one's right hand' (27:15-16). The sweet fragrance of a kind and gentle spirit permeates the air around some women, and they make the best wives.

4. She Maintains a Hopeful Outlook.

There is something eternally positive about a wise and godly woman. She finds joy in performing even mundane tasks, for she 'works with willing hands' (31:13). She diligently goes about her labours, girding herself with strength, and 'she perceives that her merchandise is profitable' (31:18). By planning ahead and trusting the Lord, she is not fretful about what tomorrow holds: 'She is not afraid of snow for her household' (31:21). Undergirded by her faith, and undaunted by the uncertainty of life, 'she laughs at the time to come' (31:25). As Matthew Henry says, 'she enjoys a constancy and firmness of mind, has spirit to bear up under many crosses and disappointments.'[1] Her unshakeable confidence in the Lord gives her resilience and genuine peace that transcend natural optimism. Her faith enables her to maintain a positive, cheerful attitude, and that choice makes all the difference in life. She understands that 'the cheerful of heart has a continual feast' (15:15).

Most marriages begin well, but over time cracks may appear in the foundation. Isaac and Rebekah had one of the greatest romances in all of the Bible, but late in life they seem to have grown apart. Isaac loved one of the children—Esau and his outdoor activities—while Rebekah loved the other son—Jacob and his quieter occupation (*Gen.* 25). It takes a constant infusion of grace and a vigilant commitment to maintaining the relationship for a marriage to prosper over a lifetime. The marriage itself must be life's primary relationship, being both guarded and treasured.

I have seen many examples of strong marriages, but the best I have seen is that of my in-laws, Jim and Ann Edwards. Having been married now for fifty-six years, they have a solidarity and mutual love that is rare. The joy they find in each other is tangible, with eyes that still sparkle when the other enters the room. I attribute their marital prosperity in large part to Ann, who displays all the qualities extolled in Proverbs 31. She is a great wife, and embodies all that is noble and good in a life companion. Like the beautiful home they occupy, Ann understands that her marriage itself is a fine house that she builds with her own hands. Their stately home, appropriately named 'O Be Joyful', is nothing compared to the splendour of their marriage.

In many ways, I am a direct beneficiary of Ann's wifely wisdom and skill, because Cathy has learned from her example. The attitudes and qualities which Ann exhibited, Cathy has emulated.

[1] *Matthew Henry*, p. 789.

At the risk of making a dangerous comparison, I remember one of my father-in-law's Labrador Retrievers, Gabriel, teaching one of his puppies, Joshua, how to retrieve ducks. (Note the saintly names of these dogs—perhaps a futile hope they would live up to some sort of nobility and virtue!) Even as a six-month-old pup, Joshua just followed Gabriel around and caught on to the duck-hunting routine very quickly. Like father, like son. Like mother, like daughter.

Marital bliss, by God's grace, is no accident, but a proof that God's instructions are light and life to those who follow in them. Of all the earthly blessings I have received, my marriage to Cathy is, hands down, the one I treasure most. My deepest prayer for many years has been that each of my children will find, and be, the kind of godly spouse portrayed in Proverbs. Next to their salvation, that is life's greatest blessing.

Mother, May I?

Mothers share the same responsibilities described in Chapter 14 to raise their children in the fear and discipline of the Lord. Every mother is to be a provider, teacher, disciplinarian, and friend.

• 'She rises while it is yet night and provides food for her household and portions for her maidens' (31:15). She is diligent about knowing the condition of her flock and meeting their needs. She is self-sacrificing as to her own comfort and sleep. There can be monotony and frustration in the thankless, repetitive job of preparing meals and cleaning dishes, unless a mother takes a very long-term view of her calling. A wise mother views the children, not the food, as the project in hand.

• 'Hear, my son, your father's instruction, and forsake not your mother's teaching' (1:8). A child is doubly blessed who has both father and mother coaching him along.

• 'A foolish son is a sorrow to his mother' (10:1). Without using guilt as the default means of motivating her children, a mother should communicate that their wisdom is a joy and their foolishness a grief to her. Teach them to consider the impact of their actions on others.

• 'The rod and reproof give wisdom, but a child left to himself brings shame to his mother' (29:15). A mother's tender heart can fall into the trap of wanting to spoil her child. Mother and child should both learn that a child who always gets his own way will find professors, bosses and judges greatly unimpressed.

• 'Her children rise up and call her blessed' (31:28). The pattern of blessing mom should be instilled in the children by their father at an early age. When they finally begin to do it of their own accord, it is sweet music to the ear. Praise and gratitude are hard-earned rewards for years of mothering, but they are worth it. Ask any mother.

Summary

Being a wife and mother are high callings. An excellent wife is a great blessing to her husband and children, and the woman who builds her home diligently will receive great honour and praise. The pattern of self-sacrifice is profoundly significant, and ironically yields the richest harvest of lasting satisifaction.

Key Principle: A wise woman builds her home, knowing it yields eternal blessings for herself and her family.

16

WICKEDNESS AND EVIL

Scripture has much to teach us on the subject of evil. The forces of darkness, under the leadership of Satan, the enemy of our souls, operate in the spiritual realm. Paul wrote, 'For we do not wrestle against flesh and blood, but against . . . the spiritual forces of evil in the heavenly places' (*Eph.* 6:12). There is a very real, but unseen, conflict raging between good and evil. It has a direct impact on us, and we are admonished to stand firm in resisting evil.

But it is not evil at the cosmic level that Proverbs addresses. Proverbs focuses on what I would call personal evil: wickedness carried out in the context of human relationships. Such personal evil is certainly motivated by the power of sin in our lives. But it is this tangible evil—the things I do, say, or think about others—that I am admonished to avoid.

A good definition of evil is the intention to harm another's person, property or name. Notice that actual harm is not needed. Merely the plan or desire to harm another is evil. And Proverbs will show us clearly the end result of such behaviour.

The sheer number of proverbs that deal with wickedness and evil tells us that God cares a great deal about this subject. The Hebrew word for evil appears more than fifty times in Proverbs. It comes

It comes from a word that conveys the idea of something spoiled or rotten. The Hebrew word for wicked appears nearly one hundred times in Proverbs. It comes from a word that means to be emphatically wrong. The evil person is broken in a sense; he is not living up to his original design. The wicked person not merely does wrong, he is wrong, and mortally so!

Deliver Us from Evil

Proverbs tells us that God's command to walk in his ways is for a specific purpose: to deliver his children from evil. Those who follow his commandments are wise; those who ignore them are fools.

• 'For wisdom will come into your heart, and knowledge will be pleasant to your soul . . . delivering you from the way of evil, from men of perverted speech, who forsake the paths of uprightness to walk in the ways of darkness, who rejoice in doing evil and delight in the perverseness of evil' (2:10, 12-14). The wise person walks a straight path and does not try to deceive. The wicked person delights in following a dark, twisted path.

• 'Be not wise in your own eyes; fear the Lord, and turn away from evil' (3:7). Though we are all capable of falling, the power of sin is broken when we submit to the Lord. We can have only one master, and light and darkness are mutually exclusive as masters.

• 'There are six things that the Lord hates, seven that are an abomination to him . . . hands that shed innocent blood, a heart that devises wicked plans, feet that make haste to run to evil' (6:16-18). The Hebrew word for abomination means disgusting, utterly abhorrent. Every form of wickedness is repulsive to the Lord.

• 'One who is wise is cautious and turns away from evil, but a fool is reckless and careless' (14:16). A wise person heeds the warning and turns back from the cliff, while a fool rushes forward and is destroyed.

• 'The fear of the LORD leads to life, and whoever has it rests satisfied; he will not be visited by harm' (19:23). The Lord actively guards and keeps those who trust in him.

• 'The prudent sees danger and hides himself, but the simple go on and suffer for it' (27:12). Like a ticking bomb, evil can explode in your face at any moment. Cast it as far from you as possible.

Hear No Evil, See No Evil, Speak No Evil

Proverbs admonishes us to avoid every form of evil—whether in word, deed or even thought. To some degree these are inter-related, because every evil action or word begins with an evil thought. Yet the distinction is important, as we will see shortly, because the punishment will fit the crime.

Evil deeds include any acts of violence or theft:

• 'My son, if sinners entice you, do not consent. If they say, "Come with us, let us lie in wait for blood . . . we shall find all precious goods, we shall fill our houses with plunder", my son, do not walk in the way with them . . . for their feet run to evil, and they make haste to shed blood' (1:10, 13-16). Beware the company you keep. The wicked can be relentless in their persuasions, wearing down the naïve. Have nothing to do with them. The problem with violent gangs is the camaraderie they offer to lonely or insecure young people.

• 'Do not contend with a man for no reason, when he has done you no harm. Do not envy a man of violence and do not choose any of his ways' (3:30-31). Violence is particularly abhorrent to the Lord, yet our culture has made violence a prized form of entertainment. Graphic video games like *Mortal Kombat* glorify violence, rap artists feed a culture of abuse and exploitation, and television producers and film makers keep pushing back the boundaries of propriety, producing more graphic and titillating material at every opportunity.

• 'Do not enter the path of the wicked, and do not walk in the way of the evil. Avoid it; do not go on it; turn away from it and pass on. For they cannot sleep unless they have done wrong; they are robbed of sleep unless they have made someone stumble. For they eat the bread of wickedness and drink the wine of violence' (4:14-17). A person who yields to evil becomes ensnared by it, and becomes obsessed with it. There is a diminishing return to the initial thrill of violence, and it becomes the very food and drink of those who 'eat the bread of wickedness'. Like Brer Rabbit and the Tar Baby, it will never let you go.

• 'The wicked accepts a bribe in secret to pervert the ways of justice' (17:23).

• 'If one is burdened with the blood of another, he will be a fugitive until death; let no one help him' (28:17).

Evil words are easy to define and are strongly warned against:

• 'A worthless person, a wicked man, goes about with crooked speech . . . continually sowing discord' (6:12-14).

• 'There are six things that the LORD hates, seven that are an abomination to him . . . a lying tongue . . . a false witness who breathes out lies, and one who sows discord among brothers' (6:16-18).

• 'Blessings are on the head of the righteous, but the mouth of the wicked conceals violence' (10:6).

• 'An evil man is ensnared by the transgression of his lips, but the righteous escapes from trouble' (12:13).

• 'An evildoer listens to wicked lips, and a liar gives ear to a mischievous tongue' (17:4).

• 'A man . . . with a dishonest tongue falls into calamity' (17:20b).

Evil thoughts are sinful, including the scheming or desiring to do evil:

• 'Do they not go astray who devise evil?' (14:22a).

• 'Deceit is in the heart of those who devise evil, but those who plan peace have joy' (12:20).

• 'The thoughts of the wicked are an abomination to the LORD, but gracious words are pure' (15:26).

• 'A man of crooked heart does not discover good' (17:20a).

• 'The soul of the wicked desires evil; his neighbour finds no mercy in his eyes' (21:10).

• 'The sacrifice of the wicked is an abomination; how much more when he brings it with evil intent' (21:27).

• 'Be not envious of evil men, nor desire to be with them, for their hearts devise violence, and their lips talk of trouble' (24:1-2).

• 'Whoever plans to do evil will be called a schemer. The devising of folly is sin, and the scoffer is an abomination to mankind' (24:8-9).

Back at You

Some people may do evil things just for fun, but presumably most people do evil things to get ahead. The robber wants more wealth. The liar wants to profit by hiding the truth. The rapist wants sexual gratification, even if he must take it by violence. Yet there is something very ironic about evil. It boomerangs! Those who follow the Lord's commandments and flee from evil will be safe; but those who ignore his commandments and embrace evil will be destroyed by the very evil they devise. Their own schemes will come back to haunt them!

• 'For in vain is a net spread in the sight of any bird, but these men lie in wait for their own blood; they set an ambush for their own lives. Such are the ways of everyone who is greedy for unjust gain; it takes away the life of its possessors' (1:17-19).

• 'The iniquities of the wicked ensnare him, and he is held fast in the cords of his sin. He dies for lack of discipline, and because of his great folly he is led astray' (5:22-23). Patterns of conduct become habits, and the wicked will be dragged down by his own iniquity. What goes around comes around eventually.

• 'Whoever is steadfast in righteousness will live, but he who pursues evil will die' (11:19).

• 'Be assured, an evil person will not go unpunished' (11:21).

• 'If anyone returns evil for good, evil will not depart from his house' (17:13). The classic example of personal evil plaguing one's house is found in the life of King David. The sordid story of his adulterous affair with Bathsheba, compounded by his premeditated murder of her noble husband, Uriah, is found in 2 Samuel 12. The prophet Nathan confronted David with his sin, saying, 'Why have you despised the word of the LORD, to do what is evil in his sight? . . . Thus says the LORD, "Behold, I will raise up evil against you out of your own house"' (*2 Sam.* 12: 9, 11). Sin, even when forgiven, has consequences, and what consequences David reaped! They were in the same coin as his own. The cycle of sin included the incest of David's first son Amnon with his sister Tamar; the murder of Amnon by David's third son Absalom; the rebellion of Absalom against David, including public sexual relations with his father's concubines to the deep humiliation of the king; the murder of Absalom by Joab; the rebellion of David's fourth son Adonijah against his father; and the murder of Adonijah by David's fifth son Solomon. The Lord had blessed David with many blessings, and David foolishly threw them away. The evil David pursued never stopped pursuing him all of his days.

• 'The violence of the wicked will sweep them away, because they refuse to do what is just' (21:7).

• 'Fret not yourself because of evildoers, and be not envious of the wicked, for the evil man has no future; the lamp of the wicked will be put out' (24:19-20). The wicked foolishly believe there will be no day of reckoning. When the day comes, their craftiness and persuasiveness will not be enough.

• 'Whoever digs a pit will fall into it, and a stone will come back on him who starts it rolling' (26:27). There is a sense of justice in seeing those who set traps for others caught in their own devises.

• 'Whoever misleads the upright into an evil way will fall into his own pit, but the blameless will have a goodly inheritance' (28:10).

• 'A stingy man hastens after wealth and does not know that poverty will come upon him' (28:22). The pursuit of wealth by improper means leads only to want. Why go there?

• 'An evil man is ensnared in his transgression, but a righteous man sings and rejoices' (29:6). The Lord, in his mercy, gives us freedom from our sin and a cause to sing and celebrate. Like the father of the prodigal son in Luke 15, the Lord will throw a big feast for the righteous.

Summary

The paths of good and evil are before us. Choose wisely. 'By steadfast love and faithfulness iniquity is atoned for, and by the fear of the LORD one turns away from evil' (16:6). Those who refrain from evil will be untouched by evil. Those who do evil will suffer from evil.

Key Principle: Those who do evil (any act or intention to harm another's person, property or name) will suffer evil.

17

THE FUTURE

Life is a journey, Proverbs tells us. The path will be full of twists and turns: many unexpected joys and some unforeseen troubles along the way. But the very uncertainty of the trip can sometimes lead to anxiety. Where will this road take us? How will I fare? Proverbs assures us that the future is bright and a safe arrival is guaranteed for those who walk with the Lord.

What's Eating You?

There are a host of things for travellers to worry about. Getting lost; being robbed; breaking down along the way. Life's travellers have many of the same worries. Add 'getting old' to the list, and the prospects for the future may not seem so bright. How is the believer to cope?

The fear of the unknown—life's basic uncertainty—is a common concern. Proverbs tells us the path of righteousness is the only secure route, both in terms of with whom we are travelling and where the road leads.

• 'Do not be afraid of sudden terror . . . when it comes, for the LORD will be your confidence and will keep your foot from being caught' (3:25-26). The Lord is our travelling companion, who promises never to leave us nor forsake us. Not a bad entourage!

• 'What the wicked dreads will come upon him . . . but the righteous is established forever' (10:24-25).

• 'The wicked are overthrown and are no more, but the house of the righteous will stand' (12:7).

• 'The ear that listens to life-giving reproof will dwell among the wise' (15:31).

• 'Let not your heart envy sinners, but continue in the fear of the LORD all the day. Surely there is a future, and your hope will not be cut off' (23:17-18).

• 'Know that wisdom is such to your soul; if you find it, there will be a future, and your hope will not be cut off' (24:14).

The fear of attack by our enemies or strangers who randomly try to harm us can be debilitating. Proverbs teaches us to trust rather than to fear.

• 'Do not be afraid of . . . the ruin of the wicked, when it comes, for the LORD will be your confidence and will keep your foot from being caught' (3:25-26).

• 'Disaster pursues sinners, but the righteous are rewarded with good' (13:21). The person walking with God (the 'righteous') does not need to constantly look over their shoulder. Adversity pursues sinners, but the redeemed are safe. Peace of mind and spiritual prosperity are the reward for walking with the Lord.

• 'The name of the LORD is a strong tower; the righteous man runs into it and is safe' (18:10). When danger appears along the road, the believer has a strong tower into which to run.

• 'Fret not yourself because of evildoers, and be not envious of the wicked, for the evil man has no future; the lamp of the wicked will be put out' (24:19-20).

The twin fears that life will be cut short or may last too long should never daunt us. The fear of premature death—being suddenly cut off—can be debilitating. On the other extreme, the fear of old age, with its potential loneliness, frailty and dependence on others, is even more common. Rather than focusing on the number of our days, we are warned to focus on their quality, measured by faithfulness in walking with God.

• 'For by me [wisdom] your days will be multiplied, and years will be added to your life' (9:11). The general rule is that righteous living adds years to one's life. This makes sense at even the most basic level, in that risky behaviour such as habitual, excessive drinking or making a living by violence and robbery, is forsaken when we follow 'the path of life'.

• 'The fear of the LORD prolongs life, but the years of the wicked will be short' (10:27).

• 'Strength and dignity are her clothing, and she laughs at the time to come' (31:25). It is not personal strength, found in the size of our retirement plan or the flexibility of our joints, but the blessing of the Lord, that makes old age sweet.

The fear of death itself can be a source of constant worry. What can I expect of the unknown beyond the grave? Proverbs, with the rest of Scripture, teaches the security of eternal life for the believer. But true "life" is more than what happens in eternity. It begins here and now. True life is time spent with our Creator, both in this life and in the life to come. Death, by contrast, is time spent under the shadow of sin, both in this life and for eternity. Though Proverbs primarily focuses on the land of the living, it does not ignore what happens to a person after death.

• 'Her feet go down to death; her steps follow the path to Sheol; she does not ponder the path of life; her ways wander, and she does not know it' (5:5-6). The wise person 'ponders the path of life'—considers what lies beyond the grave. The fool lives only for the present.

• 'Her house is the way to Sheol, going down to the chambers of death' (7:27). Notice that the path of sin leads naturally to death, while the path of obedience leads naturally to life. We should not be surprised, either in this life or the life to come, that we reap what we sow.

• 'When the wicked dies, his hope will perish, and the expectation of wealth perishes too' (11:7). The delusion of the wicked, that he is master of his own destiny, will end abruptly at death.

• 'The wicked is overthrown through his evildoing, but the righteous finds refuge in his death' (14:32). Life's deeds will be a ball and chain for the habitual sinner when he swims the River Jordan, but the righteous will find refuge in life's actions and choices. Heaven will be a place where we are utterly free from the effects of sin, both our own and that of others.

• 'The path of life leads upward for the prudent, that he may turn away from Sheol beneath' (15:24). The metaphor of a path leading upward, contrasted with a path leading to Sheol below, speaks volumes.

Rules for the Road

Life is a journey, and Proverbs gives us basic rules for the road:

1. Don't panic—God is in control.

The Lord in his sovereignty rules over all, and he watchfully superintends all that happens to his children. 'the LORD . . . will keep your foot from being caught' (3:26). 'The eyes of the LORD are in every place, keeping watch on the evil and the good' (15:3). 'The heart of man plans his way, but the LORD establishes his steps' (16:9). No harm can befall us that is not limited, allowed by God in his lovingkindness to benefit us in the long run and to accomplish his eternal purposes. During the Civil War, the great Confederate, Lieutenant General Thomas J. 'Stonewall' Jackson, was killed by a stray bullet fired by his own troops. Dr Robert L. Dabney, the renowned theologian and friend of the fallen general, preached his funeral service, and addressed the seeming tragedy head-on:

'God's special providence is over all his creatures, and all their actions . . . By that almighty and omniscient providence, all events are either produced; or at least permitted, limited, and overruled. There is no creature so great as to resist its power, none so minute as to evade its wisdom . . . Even when the thousand missiles of death, invisible to mortal sight, and sent forth aimless by those who launched them, shoot in inexplicable confusion over the battle-field, his eye gives each one an aim and a purpose, according to the plan of his wisdom. Thus teacheth our Saviour.'[1]

2. *Live fearlessly—all will turn out well for the believer.*

We are instructed not to let our fears hem us in. 'The way of the LORD is a stronghold to the blameless, but destruction to evildoers. The righteous will never be removed, but the wicked will not dwell in the land' (10:29-30). 'No ill befalls the righteous, but the wicked are filled with trouble' (12:21). 'The house of the wicked will be destroyed, but the tent of the upright will flourish' (14:11).

3. *The first step is the most important—commit your way to the Lord.*

The military teaches its officers to define the mission before launching an initiative. We should do the same in our spiritual life. The first step is to commit our ways to the Lord. 'Trust in the LORD with all your heart, and do not lean on your own un-derstanding. In all your ways acknowledge him, and he will make straight your paths' (3:5-6). 'Commit your work to the LORD, and your plans will be established' (16:3). I think it is a good practice to actively commit every major endeavour and new undertaking to the Lord. Just as a wedding is a ceremony of commitment of one's marriage to the Lord, moving into a new house, starting a new business, or bringing home a new child calls for a ceremony of dedication. When Bill Sweeny, J. R. Murphy, Mark Barrow and I started our law firm on July 3, 1993, we invited our minister, Dr Glen Knecht, to join us and our families and staff at the office for a brief dedication service.

[1] R. L. Dabney, *Discussions*, vol. 3 (Edinburgh: Banner of Truth, 1982), pp. 457-58.

4. *Road maps sold here.*

The Lord has given us clear guidance in his commandments. 'I have taught you the way of wisdom; I have led you in the paths of uprightness. When you walk, your step will not be hampered, and if you run, you will not stumble. Keep hold of instruction; do not let go; guard her, for she is your life' (4:11-13). 'When you walk, they [the Lord's commandments] will lead you; when you lie down, they will watch over you; and when you awake, they will talk with you. For the commandment is a lamp and the teaching a light' (6:22-23). Scripture is literally a road map, marking the best way to navigate the path of life!

5. *Stop and ask for directions.*

It is inevitable that we will run into road blocks, detours, and forks in the road. We can be like the New York Yankees baseball player, Yogi Berra, who observed sagely: 'When you get to a fork in the road, take it!' The better approach is to ask others for directions. 'Where there is no guidance, a people falls, but in an abundance of counsellors there is safety' (11:14). 'Without counsel plans fail, but with many advisers they succeed' (15:22). 'Plans are established by counsel; by wise guidance wage war' (20:18). GPS navigation systems may be helpful, but nothing can replace words of wisdom from someone who has travelled the way before us.

6. *Temporary parking only—keep moving.*

Christians ought to enjoy with gratitude the good blessings and pleasures of this life, but be ready to move on when it is time, toward the ultimate destination. Years ago, when the children were small, our family went on that classic family vacation. Our final destination was a family reunion in eastern Kentucky. But because we had little children, we decided to drive halfway, spend the night in a nice hotel, then continue the next day toward the final goal. When we arrived that first evening at the hotel, it was fabulous. The kids had been cooped up in the car for hours. Letting them swim in the pool, eat in the restaurant, and sleep in a comfortable bed was so very refreshing. But did we get up the next morning and decide to forgo the rest of the trip? We were ready to leave that wonderful oasis and move on toward the final destination. That is the way the Lord wants his children to view this life. There are sweet pleasures and great comforts in this world for our enjoyment. Use them, appreciate them, but when it's time to take leave of them, gladly set them aside and move on toward the final destination. 'My son, eat honey, for it is good, and the drippings of the honeycomb are sweet to your taste. Know that wisdom is such to your soul; if you find it, there will be a future, and your hope will not be cut off' (24:13-14). Press on, with courageous serenity and cheerful obedience, building a heart of wisdom. Adapt to change or loss without taking your eyes off the faithful Creator. 'Strength and dignity are her clothing, and she laughs at the time to come' (31:25).

Summary

The future is secure for those who are walking with the Lord!

Key Principle: Smile at the future—we do not know what it holds, but we know who holds it.

18

The Lord

It is most appropriate that this book should end with a survey of Proverbs on the subject of God himself. We learned in the introduction to Proverbs that the first steps in acquiring wisdom are to 'fear the LORD' and to walk in his ways. Now we come full circle to see that knowing God is not merely a means to an end, but a glorious end in itself. I wish I had the eloquence to describe how my heart soars with hope and joy, confidence and peace, when I behold the God of Proverbs.

Though Proverbs is not primarily a book of theology like the Law, Prophets, Gospels and Epistles, it teaches us a surprising amount about God. He is not a god; he is *the* God. What is more, he can be known. He is the God who revealed himself to the patriarchs and to Moses and to the sons of Israel, disclosing to them his personal name, Yahweh (the 'LORD'). The name of Yahweh appears over thirty times in this book.

The Lord's work of creation is described in vivid detail in Proverbs 8. Throughout the book we learn of his interest in our daily lives, as he watches carefully all the ways of the evil and the good. We see how he delights in those who walk according to his ways and how he abhors the ways of the proud, the wicked, and the violent.

The Lord is actively engaged in our daily lives. He instructs the naïve, reproves those he loves, and preserves the way of his godly ones. On the other hand, he scoffs at the scoffers, tears down the house of the proud, and overthrows the plans of the treacherous. I firmly believe that much of what we need to know about God and his ways of dealing with us is to be found in Proverbs. So much of what is helpful and necessary for life in this world and for that which is to come is written here in its wonderful pages.

Who is the Lord, and what on earth does he care about?

Maker of Heaven and Earth

The logical starting point in our quest to know God is . . . the beginning. The Lord is the creator of heaven and earth.

• 'The LORD by wisdom founded the earth' (3:19). God in his inscrutable wisdom created the world. Never buy into the theory that we evolved randomly from primordial soup!

• 'The LORD possessed me at the beginning of his work, the first of his acts of old. Ages ago I was set up, at the first, before the beginning of the earth. When there were no depths I was brought forth, when there were no springs abounding with water. Before the mountains had been shaped, before the hills, I was brought forth, before he had made the earth with its fields, or the first of the dust of the world. When he established the heavens, I was there; when he drew a circle on the face of the deep, when he made firm the skies above, when he established the fountains of the deep, when he assigned to the sea its limit, so that the waters might not transgress his command, when he marked out the foundations of the earth, then I was beside him, like a master workman, and I was daily his delight, rejoicing before him always, rejoicing in his inhabited world and delighting in the children of man' (8:22-31). By divine wisdom the Lord created the universe. This grand passage, which reminds us in many ways of Job 38, is not intended to mean that wisdom is a separate and distinct member of the Godhead. Rather, the personification of wisdom as a divine workman in Proverbs 8 and as a great lady building a house in Proverbs 9 is a literary device employed by the writer to vividly convey the creative power and infinite wisdom of God. Notice the exuberance the Lord has for his creation, rejoicing in the works of his hands and delighting himself in mankind.

• 'The LORD has made everything for its purpose, even the wicked for the day of trouble' (16:4). The sweeping scope of God's sovereignty over all things means that his enemies (and ours) can never escape his dominion. He alone is the judge and ruler of the universe.

• 'Who has ascended to heaven and come down? Who has gathered the wind in his fists? Who has wrapped up the waters in a garment? Who has established all the ends of the earth? What is his name, and what is his son's name? Surely you know! Every word of God proves true; he is a shield to those who take refuge in him' (30:4-5). God the Creator holds this world in the palm of his mighty hand—the wind in his fists, the waters in his garment—and established the foundations of the earth. He has been tested and found to be trustworthy. Therefore we can entrust ourselves to him without fear.

All-Seeing and All-Knowing

Far from being a God who created the world and turned his back upon it, God actively watches all that happens. He sees our deeds, hears our words, searches our thoughts, and weighs the secret motives of our hearts. What is more, he cares deeply about what he sees and hears!

• 'For a man's ways are before the eyes of the LORD, and he ponders all his paths' (5:21). The Lord is acquainted with all our ways—nothing is hidden from his gaze.

• 'Pride and arrogance and the way of evil and perverted speech I hate' (8:13b). God reacts strongly when he sees arrogance, evil or perversion. He hates any wicked thoughts, words, or deeds.

• 'Those of crooked heart are an abomination to the LORD, but those of blameless ways are his delight' (11:20). If the Lord hates the evil, He is equally passionate about the righteous. He delights in the blameless.

• 'The eyes of the LORD are in every place, keeping watch on the evil and the good' (15:3). Knowing that nothing—absolutely nothing—escapes his probing eyes, we have reason to 'fear the LORD'.

• 'The sacrifice of the wicked is an abomination to the LORD, but the prayer of the upright is acceptable to him' (15:8). This verse contrasts the wicked and the upright, and shows how God reacts to the religious exercises of both. He categorically rejects the sacrifice of the wicked because the worshipper is inwardly impenitent, while he accepts the prayer of the righteous. He not only hears our prayers, but he delights in them! In American jurisprudence we have the 'clean hands' doctrine, which says that those seeking equitable relief from the court must come with clean hands. The same applies in the spiritual realm.

• 'The way of the wicked is an abomination to the Lord, but he loves him who pursues righteousness' (15:9). The pursuit of righteousness does not mean we have obtained perfection, but rather that we are attempting to walk in God's ways.

• 'Sheol and Abaddon lie open before the Lord; how much more the hearts of the children of man!' (15:11). If God can see into the dark pit of the eternal abyss, he can easily look into the hearts of men. He sees and knows all.

• 'The thoughts of the wicked are an abomination to the Lord, but gracious words are pure' (15:26). He knows our plans and hears our words. We may be able to hide our inner motives from others or deceive them with carefully crafted lies, but the Lord knows better.

• 'All the ways of a man are pure in his own eyes, but the Lord weighs the spirit' (16:2). We can rationalize ourselves into believing anything we do or say is justified, but the Lord has a clear understanding of our true motives.

• 'The crucible is for silver, and the furnace is for gold, and the Lord tests hearts' (17:3). In the same manner that a craftsman refines the impurities from gold or silver, so the Lord uses the crucible of life to test and refine our hearts.

• 'Every way of a man is right in his own eyes, but the Lord weighs the heart' (21:2). The Lord knows and cares about our motives. He knows not only what we do, but why we do it.

Our Guardian, Guide, and Stay

Perhaps the most significant lesson Proverbs teaches is how actively and intimately God is involved in the day-to-day lives of his people. He is involved not just in the great matters of life but also in the small; not just occasionally, but constantly. Not only does he see and care about everything we do, but he actively sustains, protects and provides for us with the lavish love of a devoted father.

• 'Behold, I will pour out my spirit to you; I will make my words known to you' (1:23). This is one of the earliest references to the Holy Spirit, by which the Lord promises to give wisdom and knowledge to those who turn to him.

• 'For the LORD gives wisdom; from his mouth come knowledge and understanding; he stores up sound wisdom for the upright; he is a shield to those who walk in integrity, guarding the paths of justice and watching over the way of his saints' (2:6-8). The Lord does not give wisdom grudgingly, but freely, to those who ask for it and attempt to live by his commandments. The Lord actively shields and protects his children, to deliver them from the way of evil.

• 'My son, do not despise the LORD's discipline or be weary of his reproof, for the LORD reproves him whom he loves, as a father the son in whom he delights' (3:11-12). The Lord is a loving father who trains us in the way we should go, and reproves us when we depart from the path. His discipline is appropriate in measure and is intended to restore us.

• 'For the devious person is an abomination to the LORD, but the upright are in his confidence' (3:32). The Lord cannot abide the crooked man, but walks closely with the righteous. The contrast is between the twisted ways of the devious and the straight or honest ways of the person who does not try to defraud others.

• 'The LORD's curse is on the house of the wicked, but he blesses the dwelling of the righteous' (3:33). Which do I prefer, the curse or the blessing of the Lord? Not a very hard choice!

• 'Toward the scorners he is scornful, but to the humble he gives favour' (3:34). The Lord's divine favour and life-giving power are given to those who are spiritually poor. In the New Testament, James 4:6 and 1 Peter 5:5 both cite this verse: 'God opposes the proud, but gives grace to the humble.'

• 'A good man obtains favour from the LORD, but a man of evil devices he condemns' (12:2). The blessing of divine favour is again promised to those who are not devious and wicked.

X • 'In the fear of the LORD one has strong confidence, and his children will have a refuge. The fear of the LORD is a fountain of life, that one may turn away from the snares of death' (14:26-27). The Lord not only protects his children, but wants them to enjoy the strong sense that they have nothing to fear. Not self-confidence, but refuge in him, delivers us from the snares of death.

• 'The LORD tears down the house of the proud but maintains the widow's boundaries' (15:25). Similar to Proverbs 3:33, this verse contrasts the way the Lord brings down the high and mighty while protecting the defenceless poor. The exploitation of others is highly offensive to the Lord. Anyone tempted to take advantage of a weaker person should take heed.

• 'The LORD is far from the wicked, but he hears the prayer of the righteous' (15:29). The Lord turns a deaf ear to the wicked, while listening attentively to the pleas of the righteous.

• 'When a man's ways please the LORD, he makes even his enemies to be at peace with him' (16:7). Those who walk with the Lord will generally find life to be free from the external turmoil and conflict which constantly embroil the wicked. O, how I have seen this to be true among my clients!

• 'The heart of man plans his way, but the LORD establishes his steps' (16:9). Though we may plan to do this and that, the Lord is actively opening or closing doors and redirecting our steps.

• 'The name of the LORD is a strong tower; the righteous man runs into it and is safe' (18:10). The righteous are instructed to call upon the name of the Lord in times of crisis. His deliverance may come in various forms.

• 'The king's heart is a stream of water in the hand of the LORD; he turns it wherever he will' (21:1). The Lord is concerned about and involved in affairs of state as much as he is the affairs of our individual lives.

• 'The horse is made ready for the day of battle, but the victory belongs to the LORD' (21:31). We are instructed not to primarily rely on external means but to look to the Lord for victory. External means are important in their own right, but they are not our ultimate security. Ask Gideon (*Judg.* 7) or Joshua (*Josh.* 6) or Samuel (*1 Sam.* 7) how many soldiers it takes to defeat the enemy.

• 'The eyes of the LORD keep watch over knowledge, but he overthrows the words of the traitor' (22:12). The Lord will trip up those who craft lies and deception—don't even try it!

• 'If one turns away his ear from hearing the law, even his prayer is an abomination' (28:9). If we want the Lord to listen to us, we must listen to him.

• 'Whoever conceals his transgressions will not prosper, but he who confesses and forsakes them will obtain mercy' (28:13). The significance of this verse cannot be overstated. Each of us is a sinner who regularly transgresses God's laws. Yet the person who admits his faults to God and seeks forgiveness will find compassion. Concealing sin is futile. Confessing sin is freeing.

• 'Every word of God proves true; he is a shield to those who take refuge in him' (30:5). The Lord has never yet failed to uphold his covenant of grace to those who flee to him for refuge.

Summary

The Lord knows every path we take. Those who walk in his ways are blessed. Those who walk in their own way are cursed.

Key Principle: God sees everything I do.

19

THE END OF THE PATH

Last summer Cathy and I went to Highlands, North Carolina, for a weekend getaway. Wanting exercise, we purchased a hiking map, asked for directions, and soon found ourselves huffing up a mountain trail. The flowers and trees were beautiful as we marched further and further up the path. We climbed for quite a while, but seemed to be making little progress. We were beginning to wonder if it was worth the effort, or if the people in town had given us the wrong directions. Suddenly we came over a crest and the trail ended on a large granite outcrop. Spread before us was a breathtaking, panoramic view of the Great Smoky Mountains. We looked down on majestic hawks soaring from the cliffs below us. We saw a beautiful little church nestled on a ridge on the far side of the valley. What a memorable moment. What a blessing to have been given the right directions!

Life, like any journey, ends well if we start with good instructions and stick to the right path. 'My son, do not forget my teaching, but let your heart keep my commandments, for length of days and years of life and peace they will add to you . . . Trust in the LORD with all your heart, and do not lean on your own understanding.

In all your ways acknowledge him, and he will make straight your paths' (3:1-2, 5-6).

When all is said and done, my fervent hope is that my children and you the reader of this book will heed our Father's instruction. Trust in the Lord, walk in his ways, and rest solely on his wisdom and grace. You will enjoy the blessings of an abundant life. And I'll be waiting for you at the end of the path.

Key Principle: Those who fear the Lord and walk in his ways find true abundance, both in this life and in the life to come.

Appendix 1

Key Principles
for Abundant Living

Abundant Life: The fear of the Lord is the first step on the path to abundant life.

Authority and Leadership: God places authorities over us in all areas of life, to protect and guide us. Respect all authority in government, family, employment and church.

Evil: Those who do evil (any act or intention to harm another's person, property or name) will suffer evil.

Friends and Neighbours: We become like the people with whom we spend most of our time.

Food: Eat to live, don't live to eat.

Fools: A fool denies God and thinks he governs his own life; self is a terrible and dangerous master.

The Future: Smile at the future—we don't know what it holds, but we know who holds it.

Guidance: The Lord guides us by the principles revealed in his Word, by the provision or withholding of resources, by the counsel of others, and by the sanctified desires of our hearts.

Health: Godly living is good for the body and soul.

Husband and Father: A wise man is a faithful companion to his wife and a diligent mentor to his chaildren.

Justice and Equity: Justice demands that we speak for the poor, the defenceless and the oppressed.

Kindness and Mercy: Kindness is a genuine desire for the wellbeing of others, expressed in words and deeds.

Leadership: As the shepherd goes, so goes the flock.

The LORD: God sees everything that I do.

Marriage: Marriage is a relationship ordained by God for the benefit and enjoyment of mankind. It is to be held in the highest state of sanctity and honour by all persons, the married and the unmarried, in every way.

Pride: Self-praise, whether spoken or unspoken, stinks.

Self-Control: Self-control is the grace of inner strength, enabling us to do, say and think that which pleases God. Our spirit must rule over our body.

Sexual Purity: Sexual sin destroys the soul; sexual purity is a spring of life.

Success: Success is faithfully doing to completion whatever God calls me to do.

Wealth: God honours those who honour him with their wealth.

Wickedness and Evil: Those who do evil (any act or intention to harm another's person, property or name) will suffer evil.

Wife and Mother: A wise woman builds her home, knowing it yields eternal blessings for herself and her family.

Wisdom: Wisdom is the ability to see life as God sees it.

Words: Speak only the F.A.C.T.S. Let your words be Few, Apt, Calm, True, and Sweet.

Work: All lawful employments honour the Lord and dignify man. No job, done diligently and for the genuine service of God and others, will go unnoticed.

Appendix 2

Proverbs by Subject

AUTHORITY/LEADERSHIP
16:10; 16:12; 16:13; 16:14; 16:15;
19:12; 20:2; 20:8; 20:26; 20:28;
21:1; 24:21-22; 25:4-5; 26:10;
28:2; 28:12; 28:15; 28:16; 28:28;
29:2; 29:4; 29:12; 29:14; 29:26;
30:21-23; 31:4-7

FRIENDS & NEIGHBOURS
1:10-16; 3:28; 3:29; 11:12; 13:20;
14:7; 14:20-21; 16:19; 16:28;
16:29; 17:9; 17:17; 18:1; 18:19;
18:24; 19:4; 19:6; 19:7; 20:6;
21:10; 22:24-25; 24:1; 24:28-29;
25:8-9; 25:17; 26:18-19; 27:5-
6; 27:9; 27:10; 27:14; 27:17-18;
28:7; 28:23; 29:5; 29:24

FUTURE
3:5-6; 3:25-26; 10:24-25; 10:27;
12:7; 13:21; 15:31; 16:3; 23:17-18;
24:13-14; 24:19-20; 27:1; 31:25

GUIDANCE
3:5-6; 4:11-13; 6:22-23; 11:14;
12:15; 12:26; 13:1; 13:6; 13:10;
13:13; 13:14; 14:12; 15:20; 15:21;
15:22; 15:32; 19:12; 19:16; 19:20;
20:18; 24:5-6; 28:26; 29:25

HEALTH
3:1-2; 3:7-8; 12:4; 12:25; 14:30;
15:13; 15:30; 16:24; 17:22; 18:14;
19:31

HUSBAND & FATHER
1:8; 3:12; 4:1-10; 10:1; 13:1;
13:22; 13:24; 15:5; 15:20; 17:21;
18:22; 19:14; 19:18; 19:26; 20:20;
22:6; 22:15; 22:19-21; 23:13-14;
23:15-16; 23:22; 23:24-25; 27:8;
30:11; 30:17

A FATHER'S GIFT

JUSTICE AND EQUITY

1:1-3; 2:6-9; 13:23; 16:11; 17:15; 17:23; 17:26; 18:15; 18:17; 19:9; 19:28; 19:29; 20:8; 20:10; 21:3; 21:7; 21:15; 24:11-12; 24:23-25; 28:3; 28:4; 28:5; 28:21; 29:4; 29:7; 29:10; 29:13; 29:14; 29:18; 29:26; 29:27; 31:8-9

KINDNESS & MERCY

3:27; 11:17; 12:10; 16:6; 19:22; 24:17-18; 25:21-22; 31:26

THE LORD

1:23; 2:6; 2:8; 3:5-6; 3:12; 3:19; 3:26; 3:32; 3:33; 3:34; 5:21; 6:16-19; 8:22-31; 9:10; 11:20; 12:2; 14:26-27; 15:3; 15:8; 15:9; 15:11; 15:25; 15:29; 16:2; 16:4; 16:7; 16:9; 17:3; 18:10; 21:1; 21:2; 1:3; 21:31; 22:12; 28:9; 28:13; 30:4; 30:5-6

PRIDE

3:7; 6:16; 11:2; 15:25; 15:33; 16:5; 16:18; 16:19; 18:12; 18:23; 21:4; 21:24; 22:4; 25:6-7; 25:14; 25:27; 26:4-5; 26:12; 26:16; 27:2; 27:21; 28:11; 28:25-26; 29:23; 30:12-13; 30:32

SELF-CONTROL

14:34; 20:1; 23:1-3; 23:6-8; 23:20-21; 23:29-35; 25:16; 25:27; 25:28; 26:3; 26:11; 26:17; 27:7; 28:7; 31:4-7

SEXUAL PURITY

2:10,16-19; 4:23; 5:3-20; 6:23-35; 7:4-27; 9:13-18; 22:14; 23:26-28; 27:8; 27:20; 29:3; 30:18; 30:19; 30:20; 31:3

VIOLENCE & EVIL

1:17-19; 2:10,12-14; 3:7; 3:30-31; 4:14-17; 6:12-14; 6:16-18; 10:6; 11:21; 14:16; 14:19; 14:22; 15:26; 17:13; 17:20; 19:23; 19:29; 20:22; 21:7; 21:10; 21:27; 22:3; 24:1; 24:8-9; 24:19-20; 26:27; 27:12; 28:5; 28:10; 28:17; 29:6

WEALTH

1:11-19; 3:9; 6: 1-5; 10:2; 10:15; 11:1; 11:4; 11:15; 11:24; 11:28; 12:11; 13:11; 13:22; 14:11; 14:20; 14:21; 14:31; 15:6; 15:16; 15:27; 16:8; 16:16; 17:1; 17:8; 17:18; 18:11; 18:16; 19:1; 19:17; 19:22; 20:16; 20:21; 20:23; 21:6; 21:13; 21:14; 22:1; 22:2; 22:7; 22:9; 22:16; 22:22-23; 22:26-27; 22:28; 23:10; 27:13; 27:23-27; 28:6; 28:8; 28:20; 28:22; 28:24; 28:27; 30:8-9

WIFE & MOTHER

1:8; 1:10; 2:11, 16-18; 12:4; 14:1; 15:17; 17:1; 19:13; 19:14; 21:9; 21:19; 25:24; 27:15-16; 29:15; 29:17; 31:10-31

WORDS

4:24; 6:12; 6:16; 10:11; 10:19; 10:32; 11:11-13; 12:6; 12:17; 12:18; 12:19; 12:22; 12:25; 13:3; 13:5; 14:3; 14:5; 14:17; 14:25; 14:29; 15:1; 15:2; 15:4; 15:18; 15:23; 15:26; 15:28; 16:13; 16:24; 16:27; 16:28; 16:32; 17:9; 17:10; 17:14; 17:20; 17:27; 17:28; 18:2; 18:4; 18:6-7; 18:8; 18:13; 18:20; 18:21; 18:23; 19:1; 19:5;19:11; 19:19; 19:23; 19:24; 19:27; 19:28; 20:3; 20:19; 20:20; 20:25; 21:23; 21:28; 22:10; 22:11; 22:17-18; 23:9; 24:26; 25:8-10; 25:11-12; 25:15;

25:18; 25:20; 25:23; 26:2; 26:4-5;

WORDS

26:7; 26:9; 26:20-21; 26:22; 26:23-26; 26:28; 27:5-6; 28:23; 29:5; 29:8; 29:9; 29:11; 29:20; 29:22; 30:14; 30:32

WORK

6:6-11; 10:4-5; 10:26; 12:11; 12:24; 12:27; 13:4; 14:4; 14:23; 15:19; 16:26; 18:9; 19:15; 19:24; 19:26; 20:4; 20:13; 20:17; 21:5; 21:17; 21:25-26; 22:13; 22:29; 24:10; 24:27; 24:30-34; 26:10; 26:13-15; 27:18; 28:19; 30:24-26; 31:13-18; 31:27